GRAMMAR AND BEYOND

Enhanced Teacher's Manual
with CD-ROM

Paul Carne
Jenni Currie Santamaria
Elizabeth Henly
John Sparks

4

CAMBRIDGE
UNIVERSITY PRESS

CAMBRIDGE
UNIVERSITY PRESS

32 Avenue of the Americas, New York, NY 10013-2473, USA

Cambridge University Press is part of the University of Cambridge.

It furthers the University's mission by disseminating knowledge in the pursuit of education, learning and research at the highest international levels of excellence.

www.cambridge.org
Information on this title: www.cambridge.org/9781107655737

© Cambridge University Press 2014

Printed in the United States of America

A catalog record for this publication is available from the British Library.

ISBN 978-0-521-14301-1   Student's Book 4
ISBN 978-0-521-14323-3   Student's Book 4A
ISBN 978-0-521-14328-8   Student's Book 4B
ISBN 978-1-107-66314-5   Online Workbook 4
ISBN 978-1-107-60409-4   Workbook 4
ISBN 978-1-107-60410-0   Workbook 4A
ISBN 978-1-107-60411-7   Workbook 4B
ISBN 978-1-107-65573-7   Enhanced Teacher's Manual with CD-ROM 4
ISBN 978-0-521-14343-1   Class Audio CD 4
ISBN 978-1-139-06188-9   Writing Skills Interactive 4

Cambridge University Press has no responsibility for the persistence or accuracy of URLs for external or third-party internet websites referred to in this publication, and does not guarantee that any content on such websites is, or will remain, accurate or appropriate. Information regarding prices, travel timetables, and other factual information given in this work is correct at the time of first printing but Cambridge University Press does not guarantee the accuracy of such information thereafter.

It is normally necessary for written permission for copying to be obtained in advance from a publisher. The tests on the CD-ROM at the back of this book are designed to be copied and distributed in class. The normal requirements are waived here and it is not necessary to write to Cambridge University Press for permission for an individual teacher to make copies for use within his or her own classroom. Only those pages that carry the wording '© Cambridge University Press' may be copied.

Layout services: Integra

Contents

Introduction

Grammar and Beyond is a four-level grammar series for beginning- to advanced-level students of North American English. The series focuses on the most commonly used grammar structures and includes a special emphasis on the application of these structures in academic writing. There is also a special focus on authentic language use in communicative contexts.

A Unique Approach

Grammar

The grammar presented is strongly informed by the *Cambridge International Corpus*. This corpus was created from the research and analysis of over one billion words of authentic written and spoken language data gathered from college lectures, textbooks, academic essays, high school classrooms, and conversations between instructors and students. By using the *Cambridge International Corpus*, the series contributors were able to:

- Present grammar rules that reflect actual North American English.
- Describe differences between the grammar of written and spoken English.
- Focus more attention on the structures that are commonly used, and less on those that are rarely used, in both written and spoken language.

Academic Writing Skills

The structure of *Grammar and Beyond* is designed to help students make the transition from simply understanding grammar structures to actually using them accurately in writing.

Error Avoidance

Each Student's Book unit features an *Avoid Common Mistakes* section that develops awareness of the most common mistakes made by English language learners and provides practice in detecting and correcting these errors. The mistakes highlighted in this section are drawn from the *Cambridge Learner Corpus*, a database of over 135,000 essays written by non-native speakers of English.

Vocabulary

Every unit in *Grammar and Beyond* includes words from the Academic Word List (AWL), a research-based list of words and word families that appear with high frequency in academic texts. These words are introduced in the opening text of the unit, recycled in the charts and exercises, and used to support the theme throughout the unit. The same vocabulary is reviewed and practiced in the corresponding unit of *Writing Skills Interactive*.

Instructional Resources

Enhanced Teacher's Manual with CD-ROM

In addition to an audio script and answer key for the Student's Book, this book contains general teaching suggestions for applying any of the structures taught in the Student's Book to all four major skill areas.

The CD-ROM in the back of the book includes:

Grammar Presentations

- Twenty animated PowerPoint presentations offer unit-specific grammar lessons for classroom use. Their purpose is to provide engaging visual aids to help clarify complex grammatical concepts while encouraging a high level of student involvement.

Tests

- Each of the 20 ready-made unit tests consists of two parts. Part I tests the grammar points in the order presented in the unit. Part II offers a more challenging blend of the grammar. Each unit test is easy to score on a scale of 100 points by following the guidelines included in the answer key, also found on the CD-ROM. There is also an optional third part to the test that covers writing, and there is a suggested rubric for scoring the writing. In addition, there is a Midterm and Final Test with Answer Key. These tests also include an optional writing section. All of the tests are available in two formats: as a PDF (portable document format) and as a Microsoft Word document. The Word documents are provided for those instructors who wish to customize the tests.

Unit-by-Unit Teaching Suggestions

The Unit-by-Unit Teaching Suggestions include unit-specific suggestions for expansion as well as the following suggestions.

- **Tech It Up:** Tips for using technology to practice the target grammar.
- **Beware:** Troubleshooting ideas for common problems with the target grammar.
- **Interact:** Ideas for games and other group activities that provide further practice.

Communicative Activities

Photocopiable Communicative Activities that expand lessons and offer additional contextualized practice of the grammar presented in the Student's Book.

Student's Book Ancillaries

The following resources enhance the learning experience.

Class Audio CD

The Class Audio CD provides all Student's Book listening material for in-class use.

Workbook

The Workbook provides additional practice of the grammar presented in the Student's Book. All exercises can be assigned for homework or completed in class.

Writing Skills Interactive

Writing Skills Interactive is an online interactive program that provides instruction in key skills crucial for academic writing (writing effective topic sentences, avoiding sentence fragments, distinguishing between fact and opinion, etc.). The units of *Writing Skills Interactive* correspond to and build on Student's Book units through shared vocabulary and themes.

Program Highlights

- Each unit includes an animated presentation that provides interactive, dynamic instruction in the writing skill.
- Academic and content vocabulary introduced in the corresponding Student's Book unit are recycled and practiced through the use of additional theme-based contexts.
- The presentation in each *Writing Skills Interactive* unit is followed by focused practice with immediate feedback.
- The program allows students to work at their own pace and review instructional presentations as needed. It is ideal for individual practice, although it can also be used successfully in the classroom or computer lab.

General Teaching Suggestions

This guide provides a variety of strategies to use with recurring exercise types in the Student's Book. For expansion activities, technology-related activities, and useful ideas and notes developed for individual units, refer to the Unit-by-Unit Teaching Suggestions, downloadable free of charge at www.cambridge.org/grammarandbeyond.

Unit Structure

Grammar in the Real World

This section introduces the genre, target structures, and writing skills of the unit with a text written in the target genre, followed by comprehension questions. The short *Notice* activities give students the opportunity to practice points about the genre, writing skills, and grammar topics to be addressed in the unit.

Grammar Presentations

The *Grammar Presentations* provide presentations of the target structures. They address both structure and usage and offer examples that reflect the unit theme.

Grammar Application

The *Grammar Application* sections give students practice with the target grammar in a wide variety of contexts. The exercises progress from more controlled to freer practice, and incorporate the use of all four major skills (reading, writing, listening, speaking). They include pair and group activities.

Vocabulary Presentation and Application

This section highlights vocabulary relevant to the genre being addressed in the unit. A chart provides definitions and examples in context. In the *Vocabulary Application* section, students are asked to use the vocabulary in contextualized, controlled exercises, followed by an exercise where the students can apply the vocabulary in a less controlled manner.

Avoid Common Mistakes

This section presents a few of the most common learner errors associated with the target grammar. It develops students' awareness of the most common mistakes made by English language learners, while giving them practice identifying and correcting the errors in an editing exercise. The *Editing Task* asks students to find and correct errors in a text.

The information in this section is based on an extensive database of authentic student writing, so instructors can be sure that the errors indicated are truly high-frequency. If you see these mistakes in students' writing, refer them to the box in this section. The Unit-by-Unit Teaching Suggestions often provide further examples of common mistakes.

The Writing Process

The final part of each chapter deals with the actual writing task. The *About* section addresses a particular aspect of academic writing and the writing process. It includes an explanation, examples, and an exercise. In the *Pre-writing Tasks* section, there are prompts followed by an organization plan that teaches pre-writing strategies. Next, in the *Writing Task* section, a list of steps reminds students to focus on the aspects of academic writing, grammar, and vocabulary covered in the unit as they complete their writing assignment. The final task, *Peer Review*, has students exchange writing assignments and provide feedback to each other using a focused checklist.

Academic Writing Tip

The *Academic Writing Tip* contains information students can use to improve their writing both in the expression of ideas and in conforming to correct academic style guides. The *Tip* may address any number of issues, including vocabulary, grammar, or writing style.

Pre-Unit Assessment Strategies

Prior Knowledge of Target Grammar

Before you begin the unit, it is advisable to carry out a brief assessment of the students' knowledge of the grammar point to help you focus your instruction. A grammar pre-assessment helps you determine whether students understand the meaning of the structure, whether they can describe and reproduce the form, and whether they are able to integrate it into their writing and spontaneous speech. Here are some ways to help you obtain this information quickly.

- To determine whether students understand the target language, write several sentences on the board using the structure. (*The city would build a new bridge if it could get a grant from the federal government.*) Ask questions to elicit information about the meaning of the sentences: *Is this sentence about the past, present, or future? Do you think the city will build a new bridge? Does the city have the money to build a bridge? Will the city get a federal grant?*

- To understand whether students can describe and reproduce the form, ask them to identify, for example, the part of speech, verb forms, or auxiliaries of the target structure. (*What are the verbs in this sentence? What forms are they?*) Give students a short exercise with fill-in-the-blank sentences, and ask them to complete them with the target structure. *The researchers wouldn't extend the project unless new funding _____ approved. If the company allowed employees to dress casually, there _____ be a more congenial work environment.* Walk around while they are doing this and spot-check answers to assess students' familiarity with the structure.

- If most of the students are able to do the sentence completion, check their ability to use the grammar in a less controlled activity by asking a question to elicit the target language. (*What would happen if the government raised personal income taxes by 5%?*) Have them respond in writing with three to five complete sentences. Have them share their responses and then collect their work so you can assess the class as a whole. You can compile two lists: one of error-free sentences and one of sentences with errors. Tell students that they will be learning the structure in the upcoming unit. The student sentences can be presented for analysis by the whole class after you have begun teaching the structure.

- If many of your students are able to produce the structure correctly in response to your question, you can probably move more quickly through the controlled practice in the unit and spend more time focusing on the more open-ended writing and speaking activities. Tell students that although they may be familiar with the structure, the objective is to help them apply the grammar naturally in their writing and speaking.

Student Self-Assessment

Refer to the Unit-by-Unit Tips (which can be downloaded at www.cambridge.org/grammarandbeyond) for the list of the objectives for each unit. Write them on the board and ask students to copy them. Then have students do a quick self-assessment on each objective by choosing from these three options:

> ### Self-Assessment, Unit _____
> #### Objective _____
> ☐ 1. I know a lot about this and can use it easily.
> ☐ 2. I know something about this but need more practice.
> ☐ 3. I don't know very much about this.

Revisit the statements when you have completed the unit so that students can measure their progress.

Grammar in the Real World

As mentioned above, the first section of each unit introduces the writing goals of the unit. These include the genre, target structures, and related writing skills.

Students discuss the pre-reading questions and then read a text. Next, they complete a *Comprehension Check* activity. The *Notice* activities focus the students' attention on the principal goals of the unit. The following strategies can be used with this section. See the *Unit-by-Unit Teaching Suggestions* (www.cambridge.org/grammarandbeyond) for text-specific notes and vocabulary.

Before You Read

- Have students discuss the pre-reading questions in pairs or small groups. The groups can share their discussions with the class.

- Direct students' attention to the picture. Have students work in pairs. Ask them to describe the picture, or ask each other specific questions about it. (*What do you see in the picture? Who/Where are these people?*) Ask students to talk about their personal experiences or opinions related to the picture. (*What do you know about this? What do think about this?*) and also to predict the ideas in the text. (*What do you think the text will be about? What do you think the writer's opinion on the topic is?*)

- Ask the student pairs to read the title of the text and make one or two predictions about what the text might be about. Solicit a few suggestions and write them on the board. After students have read the text, ask them to compare their predictions to what they have read.

Pre-teaching the Vocabulary

Before students read, look through the text and make a list of words you think they may not know. Alternatively, use the suggested word list, with Academic Word List (AWL) vocabulary labeled, in the *Unit-by-Unit Teaching Suggestions* (www.cambridge.org/grammarandbeyond). Try one of these techniques:

- List the words on the board and ask students to discuss the meanings in small groups. Ask students for definitions. Make a note of words that students find difficult.

- Make card sets in two colors. One set will have the words and the other will have the definitions. Students can work in groups to match the words with the definitions.

- Use a free online crossword puzzle maker. Make one copy for each student pair. Give them a time limit to solve the puzzle.

Glossed Vocabulary

Paying attention to text signals, like footnotes, is an important academic skill. Therefore, you may not want to include the glossed vocabulary among the words you pre-teach. Instead, draw students' attention to the footnote numbers and encourage them to watch for them while reading. Provide any clarification students need for the glossed words.

Comprehension Check

- This exercise provides a few comprehension questions about the reading. To accommodate a variety of levels, have students complete the *Comprehension Check* individually. Some of the comprehension questions address the content of the reading directly, but some address higher-order thinking skills, for example, by asking students their opinions.
- Have the students compare their answers in pairs before you review the answers as a class. This allows less confident students a low-stress means of checking their work, while giving them more time to consider their answers.

Notice

The *Notice* activity requires students to analyze the genre, focus on a particular writing activity, and find the target grammar. The genre activities usually ask the students to break down the organizational structure, for example, by completing a chart with the causes and effects from a text. To expand upon the textbook exercise, you could try some of the following:

- Have students note genre-related expressions, such as *resulting in* or *one of the outcomes*. Explain that scanning quickly for specific words is often an effective way to find such expressions. If the activity proves difficult, you might develop a few more examples for the students to practice.
- In some cases, you may want students to try to complete the activitiy before they read the text. Ask students to share their answers. Then have students scan the article to find the correct answers.
- Have students do the activity individually. Then have them work with a partner to compare answers.
- To have the students focus on the genre, give them prompt cards with topics and put them in pairs or groups of four. For example, with the comparison/contrast genre, cards could show topics like *public transportation in two different cities* or *use of cell phones in two different countries*. Give students about five minutes to list similarities and differences and then discuss their ideas with another pair or group.

Grammar Presentations

Overview Box

Have students read the information in the overview box that precedes each set of grammar charts. Explain that this box highlights a key feature of the grammar points. Ask students what the connection is between the introductory information and the example sentences.

Grammar Charts

Explain that the grammar charts are a valuable reference. When students make mistakes, refer them to the relevant chart to self-correct. Here are some possibilities for teaching with the charts.

a. The *if* clause states the possible future cause or situation, and the main clause states the likely result.	**If** we get a tax refund this year, we are going to buy a hybrid car.
b. Future real conditional sentences offer predictions or describe possible future situations and the likely effect or result.	**If** a company does not make a profit, it **will** go bankrupt.
c. Simple present is used in the *if* clause and a modal is used in the main clause. The modal indicates the possibility of the result. *will* = it is certain *should* = it is a strong possibility *can/could* = it is possible *may/might* = it is not certain	**If** a company addresses social responsibility, it **can** result in a better public image. Companies **might** be more successful if they focus only on profit.

- Discuss each note and read the example sentences. Ask students to identify texts or conversations where they encounter the target language. For example, the future real conditional is used for predictions and possible outcomes. Elicit the target grammar by asking questions, for example, *What will the students do if tuition costs go up*?
- Write additional examples on the board for each usage note (or distribute the examples on paper to students). Ask students to work in pairs to match the usage notes from the chart with the new examples.
- Ask students to work in small groups to come up with an additional example for each note. You can make this task more challenging by asking students to incorporate the unit theme and any target vocabulary.

Additional Presentation Strategies

Prompt Cards

Put the students in small groups and give them a stack of prompt cards. The cards may have questions to elicit, for example, future real conditionals: *What will the government do if there is a leak at the nuclear power plant? How can the city solve traffic problems if the population increases?* Other card sets may have word prompts, such as verbs like *enjoy* or *advise*. Students can write sentences on the board with these verbs followed by a gerund or infinitive.

Photos and Art

Use pictures from magazines or the Internet. Have students talk about them using the target language. (*The picture shows the office of a high tech company. If somebody gets hired by this company, they will get stock options.*) Use a different picture to elicit the target language from students. (*What's happening? What will happen if something else happens?*)

Unit-by-Unit Teaching Suggestions

Refer to the tips for each unit (downloadable at www.cambridge.org/grammarandbeyond) for more information about the potential trouble spots with the specific target grammar, exceptions to the rules, and unit-specific presentation activities.

Grammar Application

This section of the unit practices the target grammar in a variety of theme-related contexts. The recurring exercise types are listed below with classroom strategies given for each. See the *Unit-by-Unit Teaching Suggestions* for specific writing, speaking, and other expansion activities, as well as suggestions for incorporating the use of technology.

Sentence Creation, Completion, Rewriting, and Combining

For these activities, students may work better in pairs. To ensure that students are processing the information, and to expand on the activities, ask them to do one or more of the following:

- explain the choice they made using information from the *Grammar Presentation*;
- ask each pair to join another pair to compare answers.

Listening Activities

Follow these steps with the listening activities.

1. Direct students to read through the activity before they listen to help prepare them for what they will hear.

2. Play the audio once all the way through at normal speed. Be sure to tell students that you will play it one more time. Then play it again, pausing when necessary to give students time to finish writing.

3. When you reach the end of the exercise, direct students to read through it again. You may want students to compare their answers with a partner's so that they can check for potential errors.

4. Review the answers together with the class, or project the exercise with an overhead or LCD projector, and complete it together.

Discussion / Interview Activities

These activities may be based on the listening exercise or may give students a chance to address the general theme of the unit. Be sure that the students receive feedback on their work. Try one or more of these techniques:

- For discussions in which students will need to produce the target structures, let students share their sentences in small groups and then complete the activity on poster paper or on a regular piece of paper, choosing at least one sentence from each member. Post the sentences around the class so that other students can circulate and see each one. Tell students to find errors and write corrections in their own notebooks. Choose global errors to put on the board and discuss with the entire class.

- Have students write sentences on the board. Ask the class to correct any errors.

- For interviews, ask volunteer pairs to present the interview in front of the class. During the term, try to get all students to do an interview presentation.

Vocabulary Presentation

Like the *Grammar Presentations*, the vocabulary presentation contains explanations on the left and example sentences on the right, with the target language in bold. To reinforce student comprehension of the vocabulary, try some of these methods:

- Discuss each usage note and read the example sentences. Ask students to identify texts or conversations where they might encounter the target language. For example, we may use cause-and-effect vocabulary when discussing the consequences of a teenager violating curfew. You can also elicit the target vocabulary by asking students questions, for example: *What are the consequences if a 16-year-old comes home three hours after his/her curfew?*

- Write additional examples on the board for each note (or distribute the examples on paper to students). Ask students to work in pairs to match the notes from the chart with the new examples.

- Give each small group a stack of vocabulary cards with the target expressions. Ask them to write one sentence with each expression. Have each group write their sentences on the board so that the class can discuss correct usage, grammar, and punctuation.

- Use prompt cards to begin group discussions using the target vocabulary. Write a situation and at least three of the target expressions on each card. (*What do you think about raising local taxes in order to build a larger zoo?*)

- Put students in small groups and have them build sentences using the target vocabulary. Give them lists of three words, one of which should be from the target list. Make some of the other words unusual, descriptive, or more academic. Students are expected to make a grammatical sentence. Then the sentences can be written on the board and reviewed.

Vocabulary Application

This section of the unit practices the target vocabulary in a theme-related context. The activities progress from more controlled to less controlled. Have the students work in pairs. To ensure that students are processing the information, and to expand on the activities, ask them to do one or more of the following:

- Explain the choices they make using information from the chart in the *Vocabulary Presentation* section.
- Ask each pair to join another pair to compare answers.
- For a discussion activity, have student pairs share their responses with other pairs. Ask students to present responses to the class.

See the *Unit-by-Unit Teaching Suggestions* for expansion activities, as well as suggestions for incorporating the use of technology.

Avoid Common Mistakes

The information in this section is based on an extensive database of authentic student writing, so you can be sure that the errors indicated are truly high frequency. This section raises students' awareness of common errors, many of which they are likely to make themselves. The *Editing Task* allows students to find and correct several errors in a passage. This exercise gives students an editing focus for their writing assignments. If you see these mistakes during unit activities (or even after you've moved on to later units), rather than correcting them yourself, refer students to the box in this section. The *Unit-by-Unit Teaching Suggestions* often provide further examples of common mistakes. After completing the *Editing Task*, students can do the following:

- Get into pairs and compare answers. Ask students to justify the answers by referring directly to the information in the *Avoid Common Mistakes* box.
- Work in pairs on a different paragraph or set of sentences containing similar errors and compare their solutions with another pair. Review the corrections as a class using a projector.

The Writing Process

The final section of the unit brings students to the writing task itself. There are four parts to this section: the *About* section, the *Pre-writing Tasks*, the *Writing Task*, and *Peer Review*.

About . . .

This section of the unit addresses a particular aspect of academic writing and the writing process, such as topic sentences. It includes an explanation, some examples, and a short exercise.

- Review the explanation and read the example sentences. Have students come up with any questions in pairs and write them on a slip of paper. Choose the questions at random and discuss answers with the class.

- Using a projector, show the students examples of student essays that you have saved from previous classes. Have the students pick out examples of the topic, such as the thesis statement.
- Give "good" and "bad" examples, for example, of a hook, a thesis statement, or a paraphrase. Let students work in pairs or small groups. Tell them to refer directly to the explanation and examples when giving their rationales.
- When the students do the exercise, have them refer to the explanation and examples. Have them share their answers with another pair or group. Ask for one example of each item to be written on the board for discussion and analysis.

Pre-writing Task

This part of *The Writing Process* section asks students to choose a topic and then organize their ideas.

Choose a Topic

To assist students in choosing a topic, the following steps can be followed if students are choosing from a list of given topics:

1. With a partner, brainstorm specific ideas that would fall under each of the given topics.
2. Share ideas in a larger group of two or three other pairs.
3. Return to the original pairs and decide on a topic. Expand upon the ideas and begin an outline.

Organize Your Ideas

Here students must do a preliminary outline, create an organizational plan, or complete an exercise relating to a part of the writing task. After completing the exercise:

- students can share their work with a partner or small group;
- students can review the work, especially an outline, during a conference with the instructor;
- the instructor can select good examples to share with the class.

Academic Writing Tip

The information in this box addresses a single aspect of college-level writing, such as quoting or paraphrasing.

Tips About Essay Writing

To expand upon the topic, students can be asked to do the following:

- Before previewing the topic, ask the class, in small groups, to come up with some key definitions (e.g. *paraphrase, plagiarism, citing a source*).
- Discuss the explanations and read the example sentences. Ask students to write down specific questions they have about the topic. After you have collected the questions, select several to ask the class. Clarify any misunderstandings.

- Provide an exercise for the class. For example, when working on using sources as in Unit 4, give the students a list of quotes with the complete source information. Ask the students to write the quotes as part of a sentence with correct punctuation and a parenthetical citation.

Tips About Vocabulary and Grammar

To practice using the target structure correctly, students can do the following:

- Discuss the notes and read the example sentences. Sometimes it is appropriate to distinguish between informal (e.g., texting or casual conversation) and formal (e.g., essay writing) usage. Ask students to identify situations where they encounter both.
- Write an additional example or two on the board. Ask students to work in pairs to write correct formal sentences using the target structure. You can make this task more challenging by asking students to incorporate vocabulary related to the unit theme.

Writing Task

Students now write the paragraph or essay. Here are some ways to reinforce the topics addressed in the unit:

- Show students examples of completed student essays or paragraphs related to the topic and genre. Draw their attention to salient features, such as the hook, thesis statement, or topic sentence. Show more than one example so they can see a variety of styles.
- Ask students to turn in or show you an outline of the planned assignment.
- Have students form small groups to present the part of their assignment that addresses the unit's target point, such as the thesis statement or the hook.
- Draw the students' attention to the *Grammar Presentation* and review the application of the grammar point.
- Ask the students to use some of the vocabulary they have learned related to the genre.
- Tell students to check the *Avoid Common Mistakes* section of the unit.
- Have students read and apply the questions in the *Peer Review* section before they turn in their completed assignment.

Assign the writing task as homework, or give students time to write an initial draft in class. If you are doing the activity in class, set a time limit to help students stay on task.

Peer Review

This section contains a checklist that guides students through a peer review of their partner's work. Students can exchange their work with a partner of their choosing, or the instructor can collect all the writing assignments and randomly redistribute them around the class. Here are some suggestions for students doing a peer review of a partner's assignment.

- Read all the peer review questions before reading a partner's assignment.
- Read the entire assignment before beginning to answer the questions.
- Ask your partner if there are sections of the writing you don't understand.
- Mark the assignment only according to the directions; write other answers to the peer review questions on a separate sheet of paper.
- Do not correct grammar or spelling mistakes in your partner's writing.
- Write or note examples of the target grammar and vocabulary, both correctly and incorrectly used.

As a follow-up exercise, the instructor can select sentences that contain errors from the essays or paragraphs to present to the class using a projector. Ideally, these errors will focus on the unit's grammar and vocabulary, but they could also include topics addressed earlier in the term.

Class Audio Script

Unit 1

Exercise 3.2: More Complex Sentences
(pp. 10–11 / track 2)

Interviewer New York City is known for its green practices, so it isn't a surprise that it has recently begun another green venture to reduce pollution. This is Sandra Reyes talking with commuters about the new bikeshare system in New York City. Today, I'm talking with Carol Campbell, who was on the planning committee for the bikeshare. Hi, Carol. Can you first tell us what a bikeshare is?

Carol Hi, Sandra. Sure. A bikeshare works like a subway because there are stations, but unlike subways, people are getting on and off bikes. The stations, you see, are the places that people can take and drop off bikes.

Interviewer I see. Who uses it and why?

Carol Quite frankly, I see people of all ages. It's quicker and cheaper than mass transit. It's also great exercise.

Interviewer Can anyone take a bike?

Carol Well, not exactly. You need to become a member. It's extremely affordable, though. It costs much less than taking the subway or bus every day. You can even sign up online.

Interviewer What if there's an accident or your bike is stolen?

Carol Not a problem. The program has 24/7 customer service, too. They're always available to answer questions or help you in case of a flat tire or accident.

Interviewer That's great to know! Bikeshares sound like a wonderful alternative to the regular forms of transportation.

Carol They are when they work well. But sometimes they don't.

Interviewer Tell me more about that.

Carol Well, in order for the program to be successful, there need to be enough bikes and stations all over. In other words, it has to be competitive with other modes of transportation.

Interviewer It seems to me that the program would be especially good during rush-hour traffic.

Carol Actually, during rush hour, there sometimes aren't enough bikes, or the bike stations are full. That's the challenge for cities – finding the right number of both that suits the demand. Some cities even have an app that riders can use to find available bikes or spaces at stations.

Interviewer Really? There's an app for that? That's incredible. Who wouldn't want to hop on a bike? Especially when it's so easy?

Carol Well, some people don't like riding a bike with the name of a company on it. They don't like to feel like an advertisement for that company. But, in general, I'd say that most people don't mind.

Interviewer Thanks, Carol. It sounds like a great program.

Unit 2

Exercise 2.3: More Subordinators and Prepositions that Show Cause, Reason, or Purpose
A (pp. 22–23 / track 3)

Interviewer Today I'm interviewing people on their buying habits. With me now is Roger. Hello, Roger. Thank you for taking the time to do this interview. My first question is very general. Do you sometimes go shopping when you don't need anything in particular?

Roger Yes, definitely. I didn't really need anything today, but as you can see, I've bought quite a few things.

Interviewer Yes, I see that. Why do you think that is?

Roger Well, because I like to shop. I'm happy when I'm shopping.

Interviewer How do you control your spending?

Roger I have a budget. I don't allow myself to spend more than a certain amount.

Interviewer And do you use a credit card or debit card for your purchases?

Roger I generally use a credit card.

Interviewer If you don't mind my asking, why?

Roger Well, for one thing, I want to avoid debit card fees.

Interviewer I see. Let's talk about expensive purchases now. When you have to buy an expensive product, for example, a computer, how do you choose a product?

Roger Carefully. Ever since I had a bad experience, I do very careful research. I bought a computer without checking into it, and it stopped working after a few months.

Interviewer You have to be careful as a consumer these days. My next question has to do with food. Do you eat out a lot?

Roger No, I don't.

Interviewer Can you tell me why?

Roger Because of my profession. I'm a chef. I prefer to stay at home and cook. Even though I spend my day in the kitchen, it's still nice to cook at home with a few friends.

Interviewer That's understandable, then. Well, that's all the questions I have. Thank you for sharing your buying habits with us, Roger. I'm sure many listeners can identify with you.

Roger My pleasure.

Unit 3

Exercise 3.2: More Present and Future Unreal Conditionals

A (p. 42 / track 4)

Host   Good evening. I'm Todd Richter, and you're listening to *Seattle at Its Best*. Tonight our guest is Rachel Adams. She's going to talk about how important it is for all of us to help our communities. Welcome to the show, Rachel.

Rachel   It's great to be here, Todd. Thanks for having me.

Host   So, tell us, what is one thing more people should be doing to help our communities be great places to live?

Rachel   Well, let's start with something people can do at home. More people have to start recycling their old electronic devices responsibly at a recycling center. Dumping them in their household trash is very bad for the environment. Recycling things like computers and cell phones will keep dangerous toxins out of the environment and absolutely have a huge impact on the environment.

Host   OK. Good idea. There's a link on our website to a recycling center for you listeners.

Rachel   Another thing more people need to do is to donate clothes and food to community organizations. Many people are struggling financially these days. These organizations can get the clothing and food to the families who really need them.

Host   Great ideas! What about volunteering?

Rachel   There are tons of volunteer jobs. Schools, for instance, are always looking for volunteers to help young children with their homework after school. This type of work can help a child do better in school. More volunteers means that more children would improve their grades. That's a good enough reason to volunteer, don't you think?

Host   It sure is. What about teenagers? Can they volunteer, too?

Rachel   Why not! Parks and community centers would love to have teenage volunteers. For teenagers, volunteering is a wonderful way to discover their talents and learn new skills. And, of course, it's great to put on a college application.

Host   OK. Finally, what about those of us who're too busy to volunteer? What can we do?

Rachel   Give money! Many community organizations often don't have enough money. More people need to give money. With more money, these organizations can buy more supplies for their programs.

Host   Thank you so much, Rachel. That ends our program.

Unit 4

Exercise 2.1: *-ing* Participle Phrases That Show Effect

A (p. 53 / track 5)

There are several major benefits to wind power. One is that wind power costs about the same as coal or oil per kilowatt-hour. This makes it an affordable source of alternative energy. We're now working on the technology. The costs will decline even more as technology improves. This is very important because most of the cost of wind power is in manufacturing the actual turbines. Once the wind turbines are in place, there will be little cost to maintain them, and wind power is free.

Another benefit of wind power is it's a sustainable source of energy and a clean source of energy. Wind power generation produces zero carbon dioxide emissions. This means that we should see a reduction in air pollution. Finally, wind power is also renewable. This means that it's a steady source of power. All in all, wind power appears to be an excellent alternative to fossil fuels. However, to be honest, there are some problems with wind power that opponents like to point out. We feel certain that we can eliminate any concerns in the near future.

Unit 5

Exercise 3.2: Comparatives with *As . . . As*

A (p. 72 / track 6)

Welcome, sports fans! Today we're going to talk about two famous sisters in sports history. Of course, we're talking about Venus and Serena Williams. Let's face it, having one person in your family play professional tennis successfully is incredibly rare . . . but imagine two, and then imagine that they dominate the sport! Venus and Serena became professional tennis stars in the 1990s and continue to be a very important part of U.S. sports. But who are they? To be fair to both, let's discuss each one in turn.

Let's talk about the older Williams, Venus, first. She was born in Lynwood, California, on June 17, 1980. She's physically intimidating, standing six feet one inch, with overpowering strength. She turned professional in 1994 and had an astonishing year in 2000 when she won the singles titles at Wimbledon and the U.S. Open. To top off that amazing year, she also won at the Olympics and was named Sportswoman of the Year by *Sports Illustrated* magazine. In 2001, she won again at Wimbledon and at the U.S. Open. She made it a family matter by beating her sister Serena in the finals of the U.S. Open that year! Venus won the Australian Open singles in 2003. Since then, she's also won Wimbledon in 2005, 2007, and 2008. In 2008, she beat Serena in the finals. Off the court, Venus is a successful businesswoman and CEO of her own interior design firm, V Starr Interiors. She also launched her own fashion line, EleVen.

Venus's sister, Serena, was born on September 26, 1981, in Saginaw, Michigan. She began playing very young, even before she started elementary school. Serena is a year younger than Venus and, at five feet ten inches, not as tall as her sister. She turned professional in 1995, and won her first U.S. Open singles title in 1999, a year before Venus, and later outperformed her sister on the court. In 2002, she won three titles: the French Open, Wimbledon, and the U.S. Open. Then in the following year, in 2003, she won the Australian Open. She also won Wimbledon in 2003, 2009, and 2010. And in 2008, once again she won the U.S. Open. Like her sister, Serena's also a successful businesswoman. She has her own line of designer clothing, called Aneres – her first name spelled backward. She's also had a successful career in advertising over the years.

Not bad at all for a pair of sisters who learned tennis as children at public courts in Compton, California, where their father taught them how to play.

Unit 6

Exercise 4.2: More Common Quantifiers
A (p. 90 / track 7)

Interviewer This is the third part in our six-part series on "Who Does the Work?" – a look at the changing roles of men and women at home and in the workplace. Today we will be talking to Dr. Johnson, a sociologist who studies gender roles. Welcome, Dr. Johnson, and thank you for taking the time to talk to us.

Dr. Johnson Thank you for having me.

Interviewer So, today's topic is about men's and women's responsibilities in the home. I think all of us would agree that the roles of men and women have changed and that there is a lot more sharing of responsibilities like cooking and laundry. For example, my wife and I work out who cooks dinner for the week and who will do the laundry, but what about society as a whole? What do studies show?

Dr. Johnson Well, men's and women's roles have changed, and you're right that there's more participation of men in housework. One of the most interesting and comprehensive studies was taken by the Bureau of Labor Statistics in 2010 on this subject. The survey looked at the way that Americans, specifically people in the United States, spent their time during the day. As you might guess, on an average day, more women than men spent time doing household activities – 84 percent of women. That's no surprise.

Interviewer No, it's not. In fact, I thought the percentage might be even higher. What about the men?

Dr. Johnson Actually, I think the percentage is quite high for men – 67 percent said that on an average day, they spent time doing things like housework, lawn care, and other household tasks.

Interviewer Really? Actually, when I think about my male friends, it seems pretty accurate. With both spouses working, what else can you do?

Dr. Johnson That may be true, but I wouldn't say that there's true equality even though typically women work almost as many hours as men in a given day. When the tasks are broken down, the percentages show that there appears to be a higher expectation for women to be more responsible. For example, in terms of cleaning and doing laundry, 49 percent of women said that they did those chores on an average day while only 20 percent of men said that they did them.

Interviewer Given that many women have full-time jobs and sometimes children to take care of, that difference in percentages is a bit frustrating.

Dr. Johnson I agree. One other interesting fact: In terms of preparing food and cleaning up, the numbers show some degree of sharing. Sixty-eight percent of women cooked the food and cleaned up, which is a little surprising. It's no longer the chore that women are responsible for.

Interviewer Hmm, that statistic seems to indicate that women can rely on men for this task. It's such a time-consuming task. That's definitely good to hear. What about men?

Dr. Johnson A whopping 41 percent said that they were involved in cooking and cleaning up.

Interviewer Well, if you include bringing home take-out as "cooking," then I can believe it. Otherwise, I'm not so sure I agree.

Dr. Johnson Even so, the statistics do appear to show a rising trend, perhaps due to economic factors as well as changes in gender equality.

Interviewer Thank you, Dr. Johnson, for sharing the results of the study.

Dr. Johnson Thank you for having me.

Unit 7

Exercise 2.3: Comparative and Superlative Adjectives and Adverbs
A (p. 102 / track 8)

Okay.... Next, let's talk about cultural differences. For now, we'll look at two basic areas – context and degree of individualism.

The first area of cultural differences is called *context*. Context refers to the type of communication style that a culture uses. Cultures can be low context or high context. In low-context cultures, communication is direct. For example, in low-context cultures like the United States and many European countries, people speak logically and directly about their ideas. They value concise words. In high-context cultures, on the other hand, the tone of voice, gestures, and people's status are just as important as words. Japan is an example of this, and so is South Korea.

The second area of cultural difference we'll talk about is collectivist cultures versus individualistic cultures. Collectivist cultures, which include much of Africa, Latin America, and Asia, value the group more highly than the individual. Personal goals in this type of culture are encouraged less, and harmony in interpersonal relationships is encouraged more. Family ties are much stronger while merit or expertise is less important. In individualistic cultures, such as the United States and England, each person's goals are more important in many ways than those of the larger group. It could be said that family ties are less strong.

People from different cultures can have misunderstandings in both areas. One of the most critical skills for people who communicate with individuals from different cultures is identifying and understanding these cultural differences.

Unit 8

Exercise 2.1: Adverb Clauses of Contrast
A (p. 117 / track 9)

Interviewer We are honored to have Julio Sanchez, a professor of business from Mexico, on our show today. He will be talking about important differences between the way North Americans and Mexicans conduct business.
Professor Sanchez, welcome. So, in your opinion, what are some differences that businesspeople from North America and Mexico need to be aware of?

Julio Well, I think the most important characteristic is that most North Americans are stricter about time than Mexicans.

Interviewer What do you mean?

Julio For example, when a North American schedules a meeting at 9:00 a.m., he or she expects people to arrive at or before 9:00. In Mexico, you can expect the person you're meeting with to arrive up to 30 minutes late. This is because personal obligations are very important in Mexico. So if something personal comes up, a person will take care of that issue even if it means being late for a meeting. In fact, unlike in North America, in more informal situations like dinner parties, guests are expected to arrive 30 minutes late. To arrive on time is inappropriate.

Interviewer I can see how this can lead to misunderstandings. What else should we know?

Julio Another important difference is that North Americans get right to business in meetings. They don't share a lot of personal information with people that they're doing business with. However, North Americans doing business in Mexico should expect to answer questions about their families, interests, and personal backgrounds.

Interviewer I see.

Julio Another thing to keep in mind is that while they don't normally share personal information, most North Americans are fairly informal with new business contacts. For example, they call each other by their first names at their first meetings. But in Mexico, you should wait until you are invited to use someone's first name. Until then, use a person's professional title, such as "Doctor." If the person doesn't have a title, use *Señor* for "Mr.," *Señora* for "Mrs.," or *Señorita* for "Miss."

Interviewer This is all great information!

Julio Thank you. Oh, I just thought of another very important difference. North Americans can be very direct in their communication style. Mexicans are somewhat less direct. So if you invite Mexican businesspeople to a dinner party, for example, they will say, "We'll see," or something along those lines even though they can't attend. They'll tell you just before the event whether or not they actually can make it.

Interviewer This is all very interesting and helpful information, Julio. I'm sure this conversation will help businesspeople from both Mexico and the United States. Thank you very much for your time.

Julio Thank you.

Unit 9

Exercise 3.2: *Used To* and *Would*
A (p. 136 / track 10)

My friends Rita and Edwin moved to the United States from a small rural town in the Dominican Republic over 10 years ago. They lived in Florida for two years. Then they moved to New York in 2008 and have lived there ever since.

When they came to New York City, life was difficult in the beginning for them, but they were both determined to do well. They didn't know much English, so every semester they enrolled in the free English classes that were offered at schools. In many of the classes, students came from all over the world. As a result, Edwin and Rita had to speak English to communicate. Every day, Edwin took advantage of this fact and always sat next to someone who spoke a different language so that he had to speak English. In the beginning, Rita was so shy that she didn't speak when the teacher called on her. Once she even began crying because she was so nervous. She had always been shy, so she never talked much to her classmates. Edwin finally found a job at a hotel through a classmate. The commute in the beginning was long. Every day, he took a crowded subway to work. Sometimes he took a bus, which was slower, but he could get a seat.

Last year, Edwin was promoted to assistant manager, and Rita found a job as a teaching assistant. They are happy with their jobs, but they still dream of a better life. For years Edwin and Rita would encourage each other by describing their own American Dream. They haven't achieved it yet, but they feel that the dream is still possible to achieve.

Unit 10

Exercise 3.1: Time Signals

(p. 152 / track 11)

I was born in Vietnam. My family moved to the United States when I was eight. For six years, I lived in San Jose, California. All our neighbors were immigrants. Every time a new immigrant family arrived, we helped them settle. We lived there for many years.

Over the next few years, I studied very hard in school. My parents taught me to value education even though they were poorly educated. Then after graduating high school, I went to college and a few years later to medical school. I now work in a hospital in the same neighborhood that I grew up in, and every day I feel happy that I can give back to my community.

I am very grateful for the life I have now. Even though it is years ago that I arrived, sometimes that first day here seems like yesterday. Years later I still remember how terrified I felt the first time I took the bus to school. Now every morning I wait for my young son's school bus to arrive and watch him get on the bus. The freedom that I still cherish is normal for him. Over the next 20 years I intend to teach my son about the values of hard work and the sacrifices that his grandparents made so that he can enjoy the world he lives in.

Unit 11

Exercise 3.2: More Classification Words and Phrases

(p. 166 / track 12)

Higher education can be classified in many ways. The College Board categorizes colleges into five types: universities, community colleges, liberal arts colleges, vocational-technical and career colleges, and finally, special interest colleges. Let's compare universities and community colleges first. What determines whether a school is considered a community college or a university? Well, generally, the two are divided by two criteria: the types of degrees available and the fields of study or programs that are offered. Universities are generally composed of three different degree programs: undergraduate, graduate, and professional. Community colleges are two-year schools. They offer associate degrees and certificates in career areas such as education, criminal justice, engineering, and the culinary arts. In contrast, universities are generally larger and offer a wider variety of majors. In addition, there's a wider variety of degrees. Students can earn several types of degrees, for example, a Bachelor of Arts or Bachelor of Science, a master's degree, or a doctorate. Another way that schools can be divided is by their funding sources. In the United States there are publicly supported schools – which generally rely on state funding – and private schools. Publicly supported schools are divided into three groups: two-year community colleges, state universities, and state colleges. As publicly supported schools, two-year community colleges provide a lot of advantages for students. Among the advantages are lower tuition and, usually, smaller class sizes. In terms of private schools, as you might think, the schools in this category are typically much more expensive because they depend on . . .

Unit 12

Exercise 2.2: Writing Definitions

A (p. 177 / track 13)

Woman OK, let's go over the definitions for our exam tomorrow.

Man OK, I'll test you first. What's the definition of *admissible evidence*?

Woman All right. Admissible evidence is the kind of evidence that juries or judges can consider in civil and criminal cases.

Man That's right. OK, next. What is *law*?

Woman Law is a system of rules that a community recognizes as regulators of behaviors and actions of people.

Man Perfect! OK, how about *testimony*?

Woman Oh, I know that one. Testimony is evidence presented orally by witnesses during trials or before grand juries.

Man That's correct. OK, now you test me.

Woman All right. What is the definition of *to appeal*?

Man Uh . . . To appeal means to ask a higher court to review a decision after a trial to determine if it was correct.

Woman Yes, that's right. How about the meaning of *to sentence*?

Man To sentence . . . To sentence means to announce a punishment to someone convicted of a crime.

Woman What about *bankruptcy*?

Man Let's see . . . Bankruptcy is a legal procedure for dealing with debt problems of individuals and businesses.

Woman Great job!

Man Thanks. Let's take a break.

Unit 13

Exercise 2.3: More Present Perfect Forms and Simple Past

(p. 194 / track 14)

More and more people want to eat fresh, locally grown food. In fact, many people who live in small towns and suburbs have started to grow their own vegetables, fruits, and herbs. Most residents of urban areas, however, live in apartments with no yards or gardens. So what can they do?

These urban dwellers have come up with some innovative ways to grow their own food. For example, rooftop gardening has become quite popular in urban areas like Los Angeles and New York City. Mark Johnson, a resident of Los Angeles, has been growing his own produce on a rooftop for five years now.

When he has a lot of one kind of food, he goes to a neighborhood swap, which is a place where he and his fellow urban farmers trade vegetables for other crops. The neighborhood swap was started about four years ago, and it's been attracting more and more participants every year since. By going to the swap, each person can try different kinds of produce rather than only what he or she has grown.

Some people bring cooked foods containing ingredients from their gardens to the swap every week. Emily Ling is one of these people. She's brought things like zucchini bread, eggplant lasagna, and corn bread weekly since it started. The neighborhood swap is so successful that Emily and her neighbors haven't bought vegetables from a grocery store in several years.

Neighborhood gardens are becoming popular in Emily's city now. Residents of a city who don't have rooftops can own a small piece of land in a garden. Neighborhood gardens are areas of land in the middle of large urban centers. People become members of the garden and receive a patch of land that they can grow food on.

Annie Suarez never enjoyed gardening and never knew much about it until she decided to try to eat more healthily a few years ago. She's been gardening at her local neighborhood garden since 2010. In the past few years, she's learned so much about gardening that she's started a gardening blog. She's been writing the blog for about a year now, and she says that her readership has been increasing steadily since she started.

Unit 14

Exercise 4.1: Vocabulary to Describe Chart Information

A (p. 212 / track 15)

At the beginning of the last school year here at Cascades High School, a group of teachers came to me to discuss the lack of energy and high absences of students. The teachers and I came to believe that these low energy levels were related to students doing too little exercise, eating poorly, sleeping too little, and watching too much TV. As a result of their concerns, we created a program that addressed their concerns. The program involved the students doing more exercise, eating better, sleeping more hours, and spending less time in front of the TV.

I'd like you now to take a look at this line graph that shows how students' energy levels went up and down during the year while participating in the program that we developed for them. The graph shows that when we started in September, most students reported that they felt a very low level of energy. During the first month of the program, there was a slight increase in energy levels so that by October, students were reporting low, rather than very low, energy levels. The graph then shows that energy levels fluctuated between low and moderate from October to December. From this, it can be inferred that students were

feeling some increase in energy, but were having a little trouble adapting to the new program.

In January, after the winter vacation, there was a slight decline in energy levels. Most students reported feeling low energy once again. It can be inferred from this that the cold weather and the rich foods that many students ate during the break contributed to their low energy. However, there was a sharp increase in energy levels in February. During that month, students actually began reporting high energy levels. This level remained steady from February to April. Then, between April and May, there was a sudden rise. Students reported very high energy levels in May. From this, I think we can conclude that the combination of decreasing time in front of the TV, increasing time doing physical activities, and increasing the number of hours students slept per night had a positive effect on their energy levels.

Unit 15

Exercise 2.2: More Adverb Clauses and Infinitives of Purpose

A (p. 223 / track 16)

Interviewer This is Jeff Osborne on *Health Matters*. Today we're talking to Cindy Friedman, who recently wrote an article on consumers' use of digital tools to maintain and even dramatically improve their health. Welcome, Cindy. Tell us how you got interested in this topic.

Cindy Well, about a year and a half ago, I was diagnosed with type 2 diabetes at the age of 26. I felt overwhelmed by the number of changes in my diet and behavior that my doctor wanted me to make. I knew there were tons of digital tools out there, so I decided to interview people to understand how they used these tools to monitor and improve their health.

Interviewer It seems like almost everyone is using some app or online tool for health reasons. In fact, did you read about that *New York Times* reporter who lost over 70 pounds using Twitter?

Cindy Really? No, I hadn't heard that. Why use Twitter?

Interviewer Well, the writer said he needed a "cheering section" to hold himself responsible for his eating at all times.

Cindy I love it! One woman I interviewed, her name is Pam, is another example of someone who's making digital technology work for her health needs. She was overweight, overstressed, and she also had serious food allergies. She's had amazing results with apps. For example, she uses an app to take pictures of her food when she's eating out.

Interviewer Why?

Cindy Well, because the app gives her an estimate

of the calories and nutritional content of the food.

Interviewer What do you mean?

Cindy She just snaps a picture of it, and the app gives her data on the fat, calories, and protein in the meal.

Interviewer I've heard of it, but I've never tried it. Does it work?

Cindy Yes, it does. Pam said it's pretty accurate, too. Actually, she uses that in combination with other things. For example, she also uses a running app. It keeps track of how long she runs in the morning and the calories she uses.

Interviewer That's fabulous. I definitely could use that app.

Cindy And that's not all, Jeff. Pam's also an active member of an online support group for people with food allergies. She's lost about 30 pounds and feels better than ever. But she's very committed to her health. And that's one of the points I want to make. The gadgets and online groups don't guarantee success. People need to commit to the digital resources so that the changes become long-term habits.

Interviewer Yes, and that's the hard part, Cindy, isn't it? Don't you think the Internet has also changed our roles with doctors, as well? I mean, we have so much information at our disposal.

Cindy That is so true. We can no longer sit there and let our doctors prescribe and diagnose our symptoms. With so much knowledge out there, how can we expect doctors to keep up with it? We have to do our part. We all know cases where doctors didn't listen to their patients, and their patients were ultimately right, don't we? It happens. In any case, in this technological age, we need to arrive at the doctor's office armed with knowledge so as not to waste time in our discussions.

Interviewer I totally agree with you. It's also very important these days when doctors are so expensive. This change in roles has got to bother some doctors, don't you think? That's a huge shift.

Cindy Honestly, I think that doctors who are serious about their profession welcome the change. They'll have to change their relationship with patients in order to keep them, I think. More and more patients may want a doctor who will work as a partner with them.

Interviewer I have a feeling that it will be tough for some doctors, especially ones who're not comfortable being challenged by patients.

Cindy I think it'll be tough for some patients, as well. Not everyone feels comfortable taking more responsibility for their health.

Interviewer I can understand that kind of thinking, too. I have enough on my mind these days with my job, family, and kids. Unfortunately, we have to stop now, but before we do, Cindy, please tell the listeners one last thing to inspire them to use digital technology to improve their health.

Cindy OK, Jeff. Here it is: Knowledge is power. It's an old saying, but it may be even more true today.

Unit 16

Exercise 3.1: Transition Words to Indicate Steps of a Solution
A (p. 242 / track 17)

Many businesses rely on workers who do all their work in front of a computer. For example, data-entry workers sit at a computer for hours every day. This habit leads to many health problems, including weight gain, back pain, neck pain, and wrist pain, among others. Here are a series of steps that companies can follow to address these health issues.

The first step is to identify the health issues of employees. One way to do this is through an online survey, which employees can complete anonymously, if they prefer. This will give you a comprehensive list of ailments and employees' feelings about their health and the impact of their ailments on their work.

Next, it's necessary to determine which strategies will address them. For example, if the problem is with weight gain, a possible strategy would be to have an onsite weight loss program and to offer discounts to health clubs in the area. If the problem is with back pain, offer workshops by certified trainers or physical therapists on ways to keep the back strong and flexible. Following that, implement the strategies. Invite workers to offer other suggestions.

Finally, evaluate the effectiveness of the solutions after six months. The management should ask employees, "Did the strategies really work? If not, what else could be done?"

If companies followed these steps, they should have healthier and happier employees.

Unit 17

Exercise 3.2: More Summarizing Information
(p. 256 / track 18)

Kim Hey, Mike.

Mike Hi, Kim. What're you doing?

Kim I'm reading an article about the most common Internet passwords.

Mike What does it say?

Kim Well, the author starts the article by saying that a website was recently hacked. She goes on to say that a data firm analyzed the passwords of the site's 30 million users and learned some interesting things about how people use passwords.

Mike So, what did the firm find out?

Kim Let's see. . . . The author believes that people need to think creatively when they create their passwords. According to the article, a good computer hacker can break one password

	a second. So the author goes on to say that people shouldn't use the same password for multiple accounts. If a hacker gets that password, he or she can have access to all the accounts that use the same password.
Mike	I know it's wrong, but I always use the same password myself.
Kim	So do I, and we're not the only ones. The author quotes one Internet user who says, "I always use the same password for everything because otherwise I can't remember them." She then lists the 10 most common passwords.
Mike	What are they?
Kim	According to the list, the tenth most common password is *abc123*.
Mike	Really?
Kim	Yeah. And the article claims that the most common password is *123456*.
Mike	That's amazing. What are some of the other ones?
Kim	Let's see. Some of the other most common passwords are *password*, *iloveyou*, and *princess*.
Mike	That's funny. Does the author have any advice for ways to create safer passwords?
Kim	Yes, she does. She describes a few things people can do to create strong passwords. One idea is to choose a line from a song or the title of a book and use the first letter of each word to make your password.
Mike	That's very clever. I like that idea. I think I'll try it.

Unit 18

Exercise 2.2: More Nonidentifying Relative Clauses
A (p. 267 / track 19)

Host	Hello, Tom Barnes here. Welcome to another edition of *Let's Talk*. We're here today with experts and parents to talk about media violence and children. To my left is Dr. Marc Richards. He works as a school psychologist. Dr. Richards, how much of a problem is media violence?
Dr. Marc Richards	It's a terrible problem. I feel strongly that exposure to violence in the media encourages young children to react violently when they're upset.
Host	I see. Does anyone here agree? Let's hear from Kevin McDonald. He has two children in elementary school.
Kevin McDonald	I think Dr. Richards is right. My two boys used to fight a lot with each other, and I think it was from the cartoons they were watching. Now, I don't let my children watch violent cartoons, and their behavior is better.

Host	This is Dr. Marcia Chan. She's a well-known child psychologist and author. Why don't you think cartoon violence affects children, Dr. Chan?
Dr. Marcia Chan	I have to say, I respectfully disagree with Dr. Richards. I don't think there's enough evidence to prove that kids are affected by cartoon violence.
Host	These are some interesting opinions. Does anyone else want to share their ideas? Yes, let's hear from Catherine Wong. What do you think?
Catherine Wong	Well, I have two teenage boys. They play violent video games all the time, but they don't behave violently. On the other hand, some of their friends who also play these games are often violent. In my opinion, I think each child has a different response to media violence.
Host	That may be true. So if parents think their children are affected by media violence, and they want to lessen the negative effect, what can they do? Yes, let's hear from Dr. Eric Lopez. He works at a children's hospital and has done a lot of research on the subject.
Dr. Eric Lopez	The parents need to have firm rules regarding what's allowed and what's not.
Host	But children still seem to find a way to play video games and watch TV when their parents aren't paying attention.
Dr. Eric Lopez	That's true. With both parents working, it can be hard. So it's also important to talk with your children, and if they act violently, discuss other ways to deal with their anger.
Host	That's great advice, Dr. Lopez. If any of our viewers has an opinion to share, please call in and let us know what you think. . . . Here's our first caller. Hello, welcome to *Let's Talk*.
Barbara Cramer	Hello, my name is Barbara Cramer. I think as consumers, we need to actively protest against violence in the media. That's all there is to it. The media provides violence because it sells. If it didn't sell, do you think anyone would create movies with violence or video games with violent content?
Host	Excellent point, Barbara. And can I ask what you do?
Barbara Cramer	Sure, I'm a spokesperson for No Violence Please, a nonprofit organization against media violence.
Host	OK. Thanks again for calling. Next caller, please. Hello, you're on *Let's Talk*.

Noah Friedman	Hi, my name is Noah Friedman.
Host	Hi, Noah. So, tell us your thoughts.
Noah Friedman	I'm a social worker. I agree with Dr. Lopez. Parents must talk to their children and answer questions, especially the young ones.
Host	Excellent advice to end on! I think everyone here would agree with you on that. Well, that's all the time we have today. Thanks so much to my guests today on *Let's Talk*. Join us next week for a discussion on the issue of year-round schooling with...

Unit 19

Exercise 2.2: More Noun Clauses with *Wh-* Words and *If/Whether*

A (p. 278 / track 20)

In the past, our options for communicating with friends were either face-to-face, over the phone, or by postal mail. Similarly, inter-office communication was conducted face-to-face, over the phone, or with paper documents. These days, we have these sources as well as many electronic sources bombarding us every waking hour. I wonder how this information overload impacts us. And I also wonder what we can do about it.

First, however, let's examine what some of the causes of information overload are. Technology is an obvious cause. We receive dozens of e-mails and text messages a day. We check Facebook, Twitter, and numerous other social networking sites. We read articles online that our friends post or send us to read. And we watch TV and videos and listen to the radio.

One reason for the existence of information overload is the ease with which people can distribute information. People tend to do this without considering whether each recipient of the information really needs it. In the workplace, for example, information used to be distributed at a face-to-face meeting and was handed out to those people who really needed to have it. Now, because information can be shared with an entire company with almost no effort or expense through the Internet, people often share information with those who may not necessarily need it.

Additionally, because anyone can create information and post it on a website, there's a lot of information out there. No one knows exactly what the daily volume of new web content is, but we do know that there is more information available today than ever before.

All of this may make you wonder what you can do to avoid being overwhelmed by information. Without getting away from technology, it's hard to avoid getting too much information. So one thing you can do is see if you can spend a portion of your day disconnected from technology.

Second, make an effort to focus on one thing at a time. If you're talking to someone, for example, don't check your cell phone for texts. If you're reading a document, don't check any other forms of communication until you have finished reading it.

Third, decide whether you really need to look at that video that your friend sent you. It's probably entertaining, but do you really need to watch it?

And finally, don't add to the problem. You should ask yourself whether you really need to send out e-mails to people who don't need them. The bottom line is that if you want to cut down on your technology use, think twice before you text, tweet, or e-mail.

Unit 20

Exercise 2.2: Future Possibilities

(p. 291 / track 21)

Lisa	Hey, Ben. Did you hear that our school is considering blocking Internet access to social networking sites in some areas of campus? Don't you agree that's crazy? How could they do that?
Ben	Maybe they should. I know I spend way too much time online chatting with friends and checking people's posts. I think blocking access could help students study more. I might even delete my account.
Lisa	That's crazy! I might even demonstrate against it.
Ben	I won't. I can see the benefits of it. If I deleted my account, I might actually see my friends more often. Right now, I don't have time to hang out with my friends because I'm always studying, sleeping, or going online.
Lisa	That's funny. Maybe you *should* delete your account.
Ben	By the way, did you hear that one of the most popular sites is due to come out with a new policy that would charge people for using some of the site's features?
Lisa	Really? No, I didn't know about that. I bet a lot of people will delete their accounts if they do that. They'll just start using a different site, don't you think?
Ben	I don't know. I think people might be prepared to pay to use the site because all their friends and photos are on it. And they don't want to go through all the trouble of moving to a different site. And, you know, there might be one good thing that could happen if more sites started asking people for money to use them.
Lisa	Really, what's that?
Ben	Well, if the site gets money from its users, then it might not have to have advertisements on the site anymore.
Lisa	That's a good point. But I still think I wouldn't use a social networking site if I had to pay for it.

Answer Key

1 Cause and Effect 1
The Environment and You

1 Grammar in the Real World

A Before You Read page 2
Answers will vary; Possible answer: Natural resources will become scarcer.

B Comprehension Check page 3
Possible answers:
1. An ecological footprint is the amount of natural resources that someone's lifestyle uses up. Taking long showers could cause a large ecological footprint, and turning the computer off could cause a small ecological footprint.
2. The loss of natural resources, higher greenhouse gas emissions, and the increased pollution of rivers and streams.
3. The meaning of the proverb is that we have an obligation to keep the environment clean because it will affect future generations. The essay and proverb are related because they are both about how we have an obligation to protect the environment for future generations.

C Notice

1 Cause and Effect Writing page 3
One of the worst effects of large ecological footprints is the loss of natural resources, such as oil, water, and wood. (lines 9–10)

Large ecological footprints also lead to higher greenhouse gas emissions. (line 17)

Another result of large ecological footprints is the increased pollution of rivers and streams. (line 21)

Effect 1: loss of natural resources
Effect 2: higher greenhouse gas emissions
Effect 3: increased pollution of rivers and streams

2 Grammar page 3
1. (Because) resources are easily accessible in
$$C$$
developed countries like the United States,
$$E$$
people in these countries tend to have large
ecological footprints.

2. (As a result), the Earth gets warmer. (lines 19–20)

3. Another result of large ecological footprints is the increased pollution of rivers and streams. (line 21). The sentence describes an effect. The word "result" signals that it is an effect.

3 The Writing Process page 3
The consequences of large ecological footprints can be disastrous. (line 8)

2 Sentence Structure: Simple and Compound Sentences

Exercise 2.1 Subjects and Verbs page 6
2. In 1998, Iceland (decided) to become independent from fossil fuels.
3. It (began) to increase its use of renewable energy sources.
4. Electricity in Iceland's homes (is generated) by geothermal springs, or it (comes) from the energy of the rivers and glaciers.
5. The water in geothermal springs (is) already hot, so Icelanders (use) it instead of fossil fuels to heat their homes.
6. Basic services such as transportation in Iceland (are) (switching) to electric vehicles, and all ships in the large fishing industry (may eventually operate) on hydrogen fuel.
7. Iceland (satisfies) its country's need for energy without relying heavily on fossil fuels.

Exercise 2.2 Fragments, Run-on Sentences, and Comma Splices

A page 7
2. (a) F	4. (a) F
(b) ✓	(b) CS
(c) F	(c) ✓
(d) ✓	5. (a) ✓
3. (a) R-O	(b) ✓
(b) ✓	(c) F
(c) ✓	

B page 7
Possible answers:
2. (a) Water pollution is a serious problem.
   (c) As a result, the quality of the water in many of our oceans, rivers, and lakes is unacceptable.
3. (a) Environmentalists are constantly trying to come up with ideas to protect the environment. Nobody knows what the environment will be like in the future.

4. (a) People are trying to protect nature in various ways.
   (b) Some people are helping to clean up the environment by driving electric cars. Others are working to preserve endangered plants and animals.
5. (c) It has negative consequences on the environment.

3 Complex Sentences

Exercise 3.1 Complex Sentences

A page 9

2. C; E; Because/Since the bald eagle showed the qualities of impressive strength and courage, it was chosen in 1782 to be the symbol for the United States. *OR* The bald eagle was chosen in 1782 to be the symbol for the United States because/since it showed the qualities of impressive strength and courage.
3. C; E; When/Because the government enacted laws that included banning the use of the pesticide DDT, the bald eagle population began to recover. *OR* The bald eagle population began to recover when/because the government enacted laws that included banning the use of the pesticide DDT.
4. E; C; In 2007, the bald eagle was taken off the Endangered Species Act's "threatened" list because/since their numbers had greatly increased since the 1960s. *OR* Because/Since the bald eagles' numbers had greatly increased since the 1960s, in 2007, it was taken off the Endangered Species Act's "threatened" list.
5. E; C; The bald eagle population may decrease once more if the habitats of the bald eagles are not protected in the future. *OR* If the habitats of the bald eagles are not protected in the future, the bald eagle population may decrease once more.
6. E; C; Some biologists are urging wind energy companies to develop safer turbines because/since the birds are sometimes killed by the blades of the wind turbines. *OR* Because/Since the birds are sometimes killed by the blades of wind turbines, some biologists are urging wind energy companies to develop safer turbines.
7. E; C; If people volunteer to clean up the habitats where eagles nest, they help protect the bald eagle. *OR* People help protect the bald eagle if they volunteer to clean up the habitats where eagles nest.

B Pair Work page 10

Answers will vary.

Exercise 3.2 More Complex Sentences
pages 10–11

Possible answers:
2. People use it because it's quicker and cheaper than mass transit.
3. If people want to use the bikes, they need to become a member.
4. When riders get a flat tire, they can call the 24/7 customer service for help.

5. If a city wants a bikeshare program to be successful, there need to be enough bikes and stations all over, and the bikeshare needs to be competitive with other means of transportation.
6. When riders in some cities want to find a bike or an empty space, they use an app.
7. Some people feel uncomfortable because they don't like riding bikes with advertising on them.

4 Common Patterns with Nouns That Show Cause

Exercise 4.1 Nouns That Show Cause

A page 13

2. good/major/main/primary; reason
3. important/major/key/significant/critical; factor
4. leading/root/underlying/major/likely/main/primary; cause
5. major/real/main/primary/biggest; reason
6. important/major/key/significant/critical; factor
7. major/real/main/primary/biggest; reason
8. leading/common/underlying/major/likely/primary; cause

B Pair Work page 13

Answers will vary.

Exercise 4.2 More Nouns That Show Cause

A page 14

Answers will vary.

B Pair Work page 14

Answers will vary.

5 Avoid Common Mistakes

Editing Task page 15

One significant cause of ocean pollution ^*is* the

accidental spilling of crude oil by large ocean-going ships.

The consequences of oil spills can be disastrous to both

plant and animal marine life. For example, oil that spills

on the surface of the water blocks oxygen from getting to

marine plant life. ~~Cause~~ *Because* oxygen is necessary for survival,

marine plants ~~die. And~~ *die, and* the fish that eat them can die as

well. In addition, oil spills can coat the feathers of marine

birds. Oil-coated birds can become weighted down,

so ^*they* cannot fly. Furthermore, oil often removes the natural

coating on marine bird feathers. As a result, the birds can

die from overexposure ~~cuz~~ *because* the coating protects them from the elements. Oil spills also affect the human food chain. This occurs ~~coz~~ *because* shellfish such as mussels and clams filter water through their bodies. If the water is polluted with oil, the flesh of the shellfish becomes polluted as ~~well. And~~ *well, and* this makes them harmful for human consumption. ~~Cause~~ *Because* oil spills affect human, animal, and plant life, many people agree that these spills ∧*are* one of the most serious environmental problems in the world today.

6 The Writing Process
About Thesis Statements

Exercise

A page 16

1. G   3. S
2. S   4. G

B page 16

a. 4   c. 1
b. 3   d. 2

Pre-writing Tasks
Choose a topic

A page 15

Answers will vary.

B Pair Work page 16

Answers will vary.

Organize Your Ideas

A page 17

Answers will vary.

B Pair Work page 17

Answers will vary.

Writing Task page 17

Answers will vary.

Peer Review

A page 17

Answers will vary.

B page 17

Answers will vary.

2 Cause and Effect 2
Consumer Behavior

1 Grammar in the Real World

A Before You Read page 18

Answers will vary; Possible answer: The key factors are physical factors, cultural and social factors, a person's self-image, and a person's own experience.

B Comprehension Check page 19

Possible answers:

1. Consumer behavior is the steps that consumers take when they want to purchase a product.
2. Being hungry is one factor that influences people to buy more. Being tired is one factor that influences people to buy less.
3. It is an important way to help people make better buying decisions.

C Notice

1 Cause and Effect Writing page 19

1. Physical factors
2. Cultural and social factors
3. A person's self-image
4. A person's experiences

2 Grammar pages 19–20

1. Many experts agree on four factors that <u>have a</u> <u>significant</u> (effect) on consumer behavior. (line 6) Memories about a certain product or place can <u>have a</u> (direct) effect on later decisions. (lines 22–23) On the other hand, if a person becomes ill eating seafood, it might <u>have a</u> (negative) effect on his or her future desire for that kind of food. (lines 24–25)
2. For example, being hungry when grocery shopping affects how people shop. (The result is that) people often buy more food than they would if they were not hungry. (lines 8–10)
3. Therefore, they might choose to drive a hybrid car (due to) its low impact on the environment. (lines 18–19)

3 The Writing Process page 20

1. ✓
2. ____
3. ____

2 Subordinators and Prepositions That Show Cause, Reason, or Purpose

Exercise 2.1 Subordinators That Show Cause, Reason, or Purpose

A page 21

2. C; E; Since it's/it is not easy to ignore advertising, consumers need to learn how to shop wisely. *OR* Consumers need to learn how to shop wisely since it's/it is not easy to ignore advertising.
3. C; E; Make a list before you leave home so that you don't/do not buy something you don't/do not need. *OR* So that you don't/do not buy something you don't/do not need, make a list before you leave home.
4. E; C; People can get into debt easily because it's/it is easy to buy things using a credit card. *OR* Because it's/it is easy to buy things using a credit card, people can get into debt easily.
5. E; C; So that children see the snack foods and ask their parents for them, stores put snack foods on low shelves. *OR* Stores put snack foods on low shelves so that children see the snack foods and ask their parents for them.
6. C; E; So people will impulsively buy products that they don't need, stores put fun items like candy and toys by the checkout counters. *OR* Stores put fun items like candy and toys by the checkout counters so people will impulsively buy products that they don't need.

B Group Work pages 21–22

Answers will vary.

Exercise 2.2 Subordinators and Prepositions That Show Cause, Reason, or Purpose page 22

2. due
3. result
4. because
5. so
6. as
7. of
8. to

Exercise 2.3 More Subordinators and Prepositions That Show Cause, Reason, or Purpose

A pages 22–23

Possible answers:
2. He has a budget so that he doesn't overspend.
3. He doesn't use a debit card because of the fees.
4. He does a lot of research as a result of a bad experience.
5. He doesn't eat out a lot due to his job.

B Pair Work page 23

Answers will vary.

3 Transition Words and Phrases That Show Effect

Exercise 3.1 Transition Words and Phrases

A page 24

2. As a consequence, children develop a desire for them.
3. As a result, children aren't/are not exposed to them.
4. Therefore, it's/it is not legal to advertise them on TV.
5. Consequently, viewers think eating snack foods will make them happy, too.

B Pair Work page 24

Answers will vary.

Exercise 3.2 More Transition Words and Phrases

A page 25

b. 3
c. 5
d. 2
e. 4

B page 25

Possible answers:
2. Some advertisements target children. As a consequence, they start to become consumers early.
3. Prices for large quantities of food are discounted. Therefore, consumers buy more than they need.
4. Advertisements often show beautiful people. As a result, consumers believe the product will make them beautiful, too.
5. Sometimes ads do not focus on the ill effects of the products. As a result, consumers sometimes buy products that might not be good for them.

C Group Work page 25

Answers will vary.

4 Common Patterns with Nouns That Show Effect

Exercise 4.1 Common Patterns with Nouns That Show Effect

A page 27

2. a positive effect on
3. A direct result can be
4. effect on
5. effect of
6. one effect of

B Pair Work page 28

Answers will vary.

Exercise 4.2 More Common Patterns with Nouns That Show Effect

A page 28

Answers will vary.

B Group Work page 28

Answers will vary.

5 Avoid Common Mistakes

Editing Task pages 29–30

Over the years, overexposure to advertising has

gradually resulted ~~on~~ *in* consumer inattention. In fact,

studies have shown that most advertisements have

little ~~affect in~~ *effect on* the average consumer. One way in which

manufacturers and retailers are responding to this problem

is by using a technique known as product placement.

Rather than spending money to produce advertisements

that consumers will ignore, companies simply place their

products in television programs or films. For example,

they have characters drink a particular brand of soda,

drive a particular type of car, or carry a certain handbag.

One example of successful product placement is the use of

Apple products in various television programs and films

over the years. Product placement must have resulted

~~on~~ *in* higher sales because ~~of~~ in 2010 Apple's products were

present in 30 percent of the year's top 33 films, including

Toy Story 3, *Iron Man 2*, and *The Social Network*. Between

2008 and 2010, the number of American homes with Apple

computers increased 9 percent. Product placement has

a second beneficial ~~affect~~ *effect*, as well. By placing products in

their shows and movies, television and film companies are

able to lower their production costs because ~~of~~ they use

products free of cost or they are paid to use a company's

products. For example, the reality TV show *My Fair

Wedding* features several jewelry and makeup brands in

each episode. Without product placement, the show's

producers might have had to purchase the jewelry and

makeup. Because *of* the inclusion of the products in the

show, the show's producers are able to use the jewelry and

makeup for free.

6 The Writing Process
About Hooks

Exercise

A page 31
2. quotation
3. unusual or surprising fact
4. definition of a key term
5. unusual or surprising fact

B Group Work page 31

Answers will vary.

Pre-writing Tasks

Choose a Topic

A page 31

Answers will vary.

B Pair Work page 31

Answers will vary.

Organize Your Ideas

A page 32

Answers will vary.

B Group Work page 32

Answers will vary.

Writing Task page 32

Answers will vary.

Peer Review

A page 33

Answers will vary.

B page 33

Answers will vary.

3 Cause and Effect 3
Social Responsibility

1 Grammar in the Real World

A Before You Read page 34

Answers will vary; Possible answer: Companies can improve
life in the community, benefit the environment, and have a
better public image.

B Comprehension Check page 35
Possible answers:
1. Corporate social responsibility can benefit the
   community when companies sponsor local events, give
   money to charities, or try to improve public policy.

2. The writer argues that it is important for companies to implement green policies because they can set an example for the community and the employees.
3. A company should focus on making positive changes in the world as well as on making money.

C Notice

1 Cause and Effect Writing page 35

2. Companies can help the environment.
3. Companies can have a better public image.

2 Grammar pages 35–36

Possible answers:

1. If a company does not make money, it will go out of business (line 2). The main clause states the effect (result). The writer is certain. The word *will* gives the certainty.
2. They argue that if more companies embraced corporate social responsibility, there would be more instances of positive social change in the world. (lines 34–35) The effect in the first paragraph seems more likely because it uses *will* while the effect in the fifth paragraph uses *would*.
3. The effect in the sentence containing the *when* clause is more likely to happen. The word *when* is more certain than *if*.

3 The Writing Process page 36

In order of importance (from least important point to most important point); *Answers will vary.*

2 Present and Future Real Conditionals

Exercise 2.1 Present Real Conditionals

A page 38

2. E; C   5. E; C
3. C; E   6. E; C
4. E; C

B page 38

2. Workers are happier and more productive if companies offer generous salaries.
3. If the government gives tax breaks to companies that donate to organizations, company donations to schools increase.
4. Employees feel good about themselves, and the community benefits if companies encourage their employees to volunteer.
5. If companies refuse to do business in countries that allow child labor, the countries that allow child labor feel more pressure to change their laws.
6. The companies help the environment and save money if they use environmentally friendly (green) technology.

C Pair Work page 39

Answers will vary.

Exercise 2.2 Future Real Conditionals

A page 39

2. e   5. c
3. b   6. a
4. g   7. d

B page 39

2. If the company donates the profit of a sandwich to a nonprofit organization, it can/could improve its public image. OR The company can/could improve its public image if it donates the profit of a sandwich to a nonprofit organization.
3. If the company has some vegetarian choices, it should attract customers who don't eat meat. OR The company should attract customers who don't eat meat if it has some vegetarian choices.
4. If the company creates a website, it may/might get more online orders. OR The company may/might get more online orders if it creates a website.
5. If the company installs energy-efficient ovens, it can/could lower its electricity bills. OR The company can/could lower its electricity bills if it installs energy-efficient ovens.
6. If the company uses bikes – not cars – to deliver food, it will save money on gas. OR The company will save money on gas if it uses bikes – not cars – to deliver food.
7. If the company buys local produce, it will show people that it supports local farmers. OR The company will show people that it supports local farmers if it buys local produce.

C Pair Work page 39

Answers will vary.

3 Present and Future Unreal Conditionals

Exercise 3.1 Present and Future Unreal Conditionals

A page 41

It always feels good to help other people and know that you are making a positive difference in someone's life. Here are a few tips to get you started. First, decide who you want to help. If you want to help your community, visit a local school and ask if they need help. The school would probably appreciate your help. If there were more volunteers in classrooms, teachers could spend more time with students who need special help. If there's a park or other public place near you that is full of trash, get a group of friends together and volunteer to clean it up. Your actions would have a huge impact. <u>If these places were cleaned up, more people would visit them.</u> As a result of all these visitors, local shops would get more business and hire more staff.

If you want to help people outside of your community or country, find an organization that sends money, supplies, and clothes to troubled areas. Your contributions are crucial. <u>If these organizations didn't get donations and help, they couldn't be as effective as they are.</u>

You could also spend your time or money helping an organization that works for a special cause like cancer or heart disease. <u>If you spent time volunteering for one of these organizations, you might learn more about the organizations and find ways to help them receive more donations.</u> These donations could be used to fund research and lead to breakthroughs or cures. <u>If you made a donation today, you would know that your money is going toward an important cause.</u>

B Pair Work page 41

Answers will vary.

Exercise 3.2 More Present and Future Unreal Conditionals

A page 42

Possible answers:

2. If more people donated their old clothes to community organizations, these organizations could give them to families who really need them.
3. If more people volunteered at schools, more children would improve their grades.
4. If teenagers volunteered, they could discover their talents, learn new skills, and put the experience on college applications.
5. If more people donated money, the organizations could buy more supplies for their programs.

B Group Work page 42

Answers will vary.

4 Common Phrases with *Unless* and *If*
Exercise 4.1 *Unless, Only If, Even If*

A page 44

2. only if
3. unless
4. Only if
5. unless
6. only if
7. unless
8. Even if

B Pair Work page 44

3. Offer an exchange first if the customer doesn't/does not appear upset and doesn't/does not ask for the money right away

5. Do not offer the customer a store credit if the product isn't/is not in good condition because we need to be able to resell it.
7. You cannot give a full cash refund if you don't/do not have approval from a manager.

Exercise 4.2 More Unless, Only If, Even If page 44

Answers will vary.

5 Avoid Common Mistakes
Editing Task page 45

If a company allows telecommuting, it can ~~creates~~ *create* a better working lifestyle for its employees and a better world. If a business ~~have~~ *has* a telecommuting program, it not only improves the environment, it also improves the quality of life for its employees. Take, for example, an employee who usually drives to the office. If he or she can ~~works~~ *work* from home a few days a week, there is one less car on the road. This reduces the levels of carbon dioxide in the air. If there is less carbon dioxide, there ~~would~~ *will* be less pollution in the future. Telecommuting also improves the communities that employees live in. Often employees are too busy to get involved in their communities. If employees spent fewer hours at the office, they ~~will~~ *would* spend more time in their communities. Employees can ~~gets~~ *get* involved in local programs if they can structure their own working days. For example, many telecommuters cannot volunteer in local schools or other neighborhood activities ~~otherwise~~ *unless* they have some free time during the week. If more companies offered telecommuting, both the environment and our communities ~~will~~ *would* benefit.

6 The Writing Process
About Paragraph Order

Exercise page 47

1. time
2. familiarity
3. sequence
4. importance

Pre-writing Tasks

Choose a Topic

A page 47

Answers will vary.

B page 47

Answers will vary.

Organize Your Ideas page 48

Answers will vary.

Writing Task page 48

Answers will vary.

Peer Review

A page 49

Answers will vary.

B page 49

Answers will vary.

4 Cause and Effect 4
Alternative Energy Sources

1 Grammar in the Real World

A Before You Read page 50

Answers will vary; Possible answer: Solar energy is feasible and a clean source of energy.

B Comprehension Check page 51

Possible answers:

1. Traditional energy sources can potentially lead to global warming, scarcity of resources, and high prices.
2. Renewable sources are clean sources of energy and are naturally replaced in the environment. An example is solar energy. Nonrenewable sources cannot be replaced, so there is a possibility that they will become scarce. Examples are coal, oil, and natural gas.
3. Yes, because solar energy is clean and does not create pollution.

C Notice

1 Cause and Effect Writing page 51

Cause		Effect
Electricity is produced by using nonrenewable fossil fuels.	→	Using nonrenewable fossil fuels can potentially lead to global warming, scarcity of resources, and high prices.
Solar energy is converted into thermal energy.	→	It provides hot water and heat for homes and offices.

Solar power output doubles.	→	The cost of solar energy decreases by 20 percent.
Solar energy uses long-lasting panels to convert energy from sunlight.	→	It reduces our use of coal, oil, and natural gas.

2 Grammar pages 51–52

1. For example, solar energy uses long-lasting solar panels to convert energy from sunlight, (thereby) reducing our dependence on coal, oil and gas. (lines 22–23) The world needs energy sources like solar energy that can save resources, (thus) preserving the environment. (lines 25–26)
2. For example, solar energy uses long-lasting solar panels to convert energy from sunlight, thereby reducing our dependence on coal, oil, and gas. (lines 22–23); As a result, it reduces our dependence on coal, oil, and gas. The world needs energy sources like solar energy that can save resources, thus preserving the environment. (lines 25–26); As a result, these sources preserve the environment.
3. The -*ing* phrase states a cause. It comes first in the sentence.

3 The Writing Process page 52

The Source	The Reporting Verb	The Expert's Ideas
ACCENT, a European research company	claims	. . . each person's energy use has risen dramatically.
Lester Brown	warns	. . . reserves of oil in the world are gradually shrinking.
Noah Kaye	points out	. . . the price of solar power decreases almost 20 percent whenever the usage doubles.

2 -*ing* Participle Phrases That Show Effect
Exercise 2.1 -*ing* Participle Phrases That Show Effect

A page 53

2. e   4. c
3. a   5. b

B page 53

2. The technology of wind power is improving, lowering the costs even further.
3. Wind power will not involve many costs in the near future, providing low cost power to everyone.

4. Wind power produces zero carbon dioxide emissions, reducing air pollution.
5. Wind energy is renewable, being a steady source of power.

Exercise 2.2 *-ing* Participle Phrases That Show Effect

A page 54

2. E; C   5. C; E
3. E; C   6. E; C
4. C; E   7. C; E

B Pair Work page 54

2. Solar cells are silent when collecting energy, thus/thereby reducing noise pollution.
3. Solar energy does not release any harmful gases into the atmosphere, thus/thereby helping keep our air clean.
4. Homeowners can sell excess electricity they create through solar energy, thus/thereby producing extra income with no extra effort.
5. Governments often give tax credits for solar power generation, thus/thereby lowering the cost of installing a solar energy system.
6. Solar energy exists in the sunlight we enjoy every day, thus/thereby providing a long-term source of energy.
7. Wind power is another clean source of energy, thus/thereby offering another renewable option for our future energy needs.

3 *-ing* Participle Phrases That Show Cause

Exercise 3.1 *-ing* Participle Phrases That Show Cause

A pages 55–56

Many people want to save energy in their homes, but they're not sure how. The truth is there are several simple ways to begin saving energy and money. First, people can keep their appliances unplugged when they're not in use, (decreasing) small amounts of energy use with each unplugged appliance. In taking that simple step, some consumers have saved hundreds of dollars in energy costs in a single year. Along the same lines, people should not leave the lights on when they're not in a room. By making this change, people can easily save a few dollars a month on their energy bills. Also, by purchasing and installing energy-efficient appliances, people can reduce their energy use. These appliances may cost more money to buy. However, they save consumers money in the long run, (using) less electricity than regular appliances. Keeping doors and windows closed, people can reduce their use of air conditioning and heating. By setting thermostats lower while they are away or sleeping, people can reduce their energy costs by up to 10 percent. All consumers should

take these simple steps, (making) a positive difference in energy use and reducing electricity bills.

B Pair Work page 56

Answers will vary.

Exercise 3.2 *-ing* Participle Phrases That Show Cause

A page 56

Answers will vary.

B Pair Work page 56

Answers will vary.

4 Verbs That Show Cause and Effect

Exercise 4.1 Common Verbs That Show Cause and Effect pages 57–58

2. Growing concerns about environmental issues contributed to the government's decision in the 1970s to promote alternative energy sources.
3. Increase in oil supplies and falling prices in the 1980s resulted from a reduction in U.S. rules requiring more fuel-efficient cars.
4. An increase in fossil fuel usage and nuclear plants was caused by a lack of consistent solar and wind energy supplies.
5. In the future, hydrogen-based energy sources could lead to pollution-free cities.
6. Continued overreliance on oil could cause political conflicts in the future.

Exercise 4.2 More Common Verbs That Show Cause and Effect

A page 58

2. was a result of   5. resulted from
3. contributed to   6. resulted in
4. produced   7. has contributed to

B Pair Work page 58

Answers will vary.

5 Avoid Common Mistakes

Editing Task page 59

Rising awareness of the dangers of carbon emissions and the limits of our natural resources has contributed ~~for~~ *to* some creative ideas for alternative energy sources. While most scientists think of ways to use renewable resources in the environment to make energy, others are finding ways to generate electricity resulting from the movements of the human body. In 2010, Michael McAlpine of Princeton University and some of his colleagues placed a material called PZT into flexible silicone rubber sheets. The PZT-filled sheets generate an electrical current when they are bent. Bending the sheets repeatedly results ~~of~~ *in* a significant amount of energy. Placing these crystals in a pair of shoes or even directly into the body could result ~~of~~ *in* enough electricity to charge devices like cell phones or tablets.

Our body heat can help create energy, too. In 2007 and 2008, Belgian nanotechnology engineers built thermoelectric devices that allow a person's body heat to contribute ~~for~~ *to* powering medical devices such as EKG machines and brain monitors. In 2010, engineers in Paris discovered a different way to use body heat to conserve electricity. The engineers developed a system that uses geothermal technology to move heat from a metro, or subway, station to heating pipes in a public-housing project above the station. Their system resulted ~~from~~ *in* a 33 percent cut in carbon dioxide emissions in the housing project's heating system. Innovative approaches like these ~~contributes~~ *contribute* to solving our ongoing need for alternative energy sources.

6 The Writing Process
About Paraphrasing

Exercise

A page 61

Answers will vary.

B Pair Work page 61

Answers will vary.

Pre-writing Tasks

Choose a Topic

A page 62

Answers will vary.

B Pair Work page 62

Answers will vary.

Organize Your Ideas

A page 62

Answers will vary.

B Pair Work page 62

Answers will vary.

Writing Task pages 62–63

Answers will vary.

Peer Review

A page 63

Answers will vary.

B page 63

Answers will vary.

5 Comparison and Contrast 1
Family Size and Personality

1 Grammar in the Real World

A Before You Read page 64

Answers will vary; Possible answer: Birth order can have a major effect on personality.

B Comprehension Check page 65

Possible answers:
1. They are the firstborn children in their families.
2. Because they are born into an environment of high expectations.
3. *Answers will vary.*

C Notice

1 Comparison and Contrast Writing page 65

2. Middle children
3. realistic
4. insightful
5. Youngest children
6. controlling
7. social
8. Only child
9. accomplished

2 Grammar page 66

1. Middle children are less determined.; *Answers will vary.*
2. They are equally creative.; *Answers will vary.*
3. They are likely to be equally intelligent.; *Answers will vary.*

3 The Writing Process page 66

Body Paragraph 1: <u>Firstborn children often share several traits.</u>

Body Paragraph 2: <u>Middle children, on the other hand, exhibit different characteristics from firstborns.</u>

Body Paragraph 3: <u>Youngest children are often more protected than their older siblings.</u>

Body Paragraph 4: <u>A child with no siblings, an "only child," also exhibits some unique characteristics.</u>

2 Identifying Relative Clauses

Exercise 2.1 Identifying Relative Clauses

A pages 68–69

2. whose
3. who/that
4. who/that
5. who/that
6. that/which
7. whom
8. who/that
9. who/that
10. that/which

B page 69

2. P
3. S
4. S
5. S
6. O
7. O
8. S
9. S
10. S

Exercise 2.2 More Identifying Relative Clauses

A page 69

2. Parents who/that want their children to excel put a lot of pressure on their children to do a lot of activities.
3. Children whose parents have high expectations of them often feel a lot of stress.
4. Sports practice and music lessons are examples of activities which/that some parents expect their children to do after school.
5. Parents who/that give proper emotional support to their children raise more independent adults.
6. Some children whose parents both work long hours have behavioral problems at school.

B Pair Work page 69

Answers will vary.

3 Comparatives with *As . . . As*

Exercise 3.1 Comparatives with *As . . . As*

A page 71

2. are not as sociable as
3. are (just) as creative as
4. are not as realistic as
5. are (just) as dependent as

6. are (just) as realistic
7. are not as creative as
8. are not as dependent as

B page 71

Answers will vary.

Exercise 3.2 Comparatives with *As . . . As*

A page 72

	Venus Williams	**Serena Williams**
1. Birth date	June 17, 1980	September 26, 1981
2. Height	6'1"	5'10"
3. Year turned professional	1994	1995
4. Wimbledon singles victories (individual years)	2000, 2001, 2005, 2007, 2008	2002, 2003, 2009, 2010
5. U.S. Open singles victories (individual years)	2000, 2001	1999, 2002, 2008

B page 72

Possible answers:

2. Serena has not played quite as long as Venus.
3. Serena is almost as old as Venus.
4. Serena has almost as much experience as Venus.
5. Serena is just as important to U.S. sports as Venus.
6. Serena has not won nearly as many Wimbledon singles as Venus.
7. Venus is just as famous as Serena.
8. Venus has not had quite as many U.S. Open singles victories as Serena.
9. Venus has had just as much success in business as Serena. They are both successful businesswomen.

C Pair Work page 72

Answers will vary.

4 Common Patterns That Show Contrast

Exercise 4.1 Vocabulary That Shows Contrast

A page 74

2. significantly different from
3. differ from
4. In contrast
5. Unlike

B Pair Work page 74

Answers will vary.

5 Avoid Common Mistakes

Editing Task page 75

A major way that families have changed is the number of families *that* have only one child. The number of families *that* had only one child was low in the United States in the 1950s and 1960s. However, one-child families began increasing in the 1970s and are very common today. This is especially true in households ~~who~~ *that* have only one parent. One reason families are smaller is the cost of living. It is not the same ~~than~~ *as* it was 40 years ago. For example, it costs about 10 times more to send a child to college than it did 40 years ago. As a result, many parents choose to have only one child because they do not have enough money for more children. In addition, attitudes about only children are also not the same ~~than~~ *as* attitudes about them in the past. In the 1950s and 1960s, people avoided having only one child. At that time, many people thought that children *who* did not have siblings had many disadvantages. For example, people thought that they did not learn good social skills. However, recent studies ~~who~~ *that* focus on only children show a different picture. These studies show that only children tend to have the same social skills ~~than~~ *as* children who ~~has~~ *have* siblings.

6 The Writing Process

About Topic Sentences

Exercise

A Pair Work page 77

1. strong
2. weak
3. strong
4. weak
5. weak

B page 77

Answers will vary.

Pre-writing Tasks

Choose a Topic

A page 77

Answers will vary.

B Pair Work page 77

Answers will vary.

Organize Your Ideas

A page 78

Answers will vary.

B Pair Work page 78

Answers will vary.

Writing Task page 79

Answers will vary.

Peer Review

A page 79

Answers will vary.

B page 79

Answers will vary.

6 Comparison and Contrast 2

Men, Women, and Equality

1 Grammar in the Real World

A Before You Read page 80

Answers will vary; Possible answer: Men and women are expected to behave differently at work. Assertive women are not as well-received as men who are assertive. Women make less money than men for the same jobs. Women are raised to be subordinate.

B Comprehension Check page 81

Possible answers:
1. Gender inequality is unequal treatment and opportunities for women. It can be found in the workplace and in society.
2. In the workplace there are fewer female CEOs and in leadership positions, and women are paid less for the same positions.
3. Boys receive blue clothes and blankets, while girls receive pink clothes and blankets. Boys are given toy cars, trucks, and soldiers, while girls are given dolls, dollhouses, and toy ovens.

C Notice

1 Comparison and Contrast Writing page 81

4. assertive; confident; decisive
5. flexible; cooperative; deferential
6. less money
7. Differences in gender roles and expectations from birth
8. cars; trucks; soldiers

9. dolls; dollhouses; toy ovens
10. aggressive; dominant
11. emotional; subordinate

2 Grammar page 82

1. Men: 3 adjectives. Women: 3 adjectives. They are both listed in a series.
2. Boys: 3 toys. Girls: 3 toys.
3. "In terms of behavior, in many cultures people tend to expect boys to be aggressive and dominant, whereas they generally expect girls to be emotional and subordinate." (lines 26–28) Boys: 2 adjectives. Girls: 2 adjectives.
   The same verb phrase is used in both clauses.

3 The Writing Process page 82

Topic sentence: Women and men are not always treated equally at work.
Supporting details: 1. "The clearest sign . . . " (line 9); 2. "Another sign of gender inequality is . . . " (line 12); 3. "There are also significant . . . " (line 17)

2 Complex Noun Phrases
Exercise 2.1 Complex Noun Phrases

A page 83

2. Today, there are more and more women (in the field of) (engineering).
3. There didn't use to be many men <u>who were attracted to the field of nursing</u>.
4. Now the number of men <u>who are working as nurses</u> is growing.
5. Two fields <u>that once were occupied only by men</u> were law enforcement and firefighting.
6. These are two careers <u>that are attracting many young women today</u>.
7. Because of an increase (in demand and services) (in data communications and home health-care aides), more men and women are choosing professions (in these areas)

B Pair Work page 84

3. There didn't use to be many men attracted to the field of nursing.
4. Now the number of men working as nurses is growing.
5. Two fields once occupied only by men were law enforcement and firefighting.
6. These are two careers attracting many young women today.

Exercise 2.2 More Noun Phrases page 84

2. achievement; progress
3. recent; growth
4. dominant; role
5. long; difficult; struggle

6. increase; participation
7. steady; rise
8. Women's; higher; enrollment
9. optimistic; perception

3 Parallel Structure
Exercise 3.1 Parallel Structure page 86

2. c. invest in their future
3. b. providing for their families
4. a. unemotional
5. b. mentors
6. c. promotions

Exercise 3.2 More Parallel Structure

A pages 86–87
Answers will vary.

B page 87
Answers will vary.

C Group Work page 87
Answers will vary.

4 Common Quantifiers
Exercise 4.1 Common Quantifiers

A page 89

2. Fewer
3. substantially more
4. A slightly higher number of
5. Significantly fewer
6. Most of

B Pair Work page 90
Answers will vary.

C Pair Work page 90
Answers will vary.

Exercise 4.2 More Common Quantifiers

A page 90
2. c   5. b
3. b   6. c
4. c

B pages 90–91
Answers will vary.

C Group Work page 91
Answers will vary.

5 Avoid Common Mistakes

Editing Task pages 91–92

Roles for women in the United States have changed

in terms of the subjects that women study in college

the careers that they choose

and ~~they choose careers~~. Before the 1970s, most middle-

pursue

class men were expected to attend college and ~~pursuing~~

well paid

careers that were both professional and ~~they paid well~~. Men

provided the main financial support for the family.

Middle-class women, however, were expected to

prepare

get married or, if they went to college, ~~preparing~~ for

traditionally female professions, such as teaching or

nursing

~~to be a nurse~~. Women were not expected to support a

family. If a woman worked after college, she was expected

had

to stop as soon as she got married or ~~to have~~ children.

Because they did not expect to support a family or

work

~~working~~ for a long time, some women also studied non-

career-oriented subjects such as literature or art history.

Nowadays, in contrast, most women plan to work for most

of their adult lives and ~~they~~ help support their families.

Many women feel that they should prepare for a job, that

that they should

they should move forward in their careers, and ~~to~~ find

satisfaction in their work. Therefore, today, there are many

more women studying career-oriented subjects such as

business, accounting, and ~~to work in~~ law enforcement. In

fact, many fields that were once thought of as for men only,

such as law enforcement, now employ women. Although

women still do not earn as much as men, they have come

a long way since the 1970s in expanding their college and

career opportunities.

6 The Writing Process
About Supporting Details

Exercise

A page 93

1. e   3. d   5. c   7. b
2. a   4. g   6. f

B page 93

1. a definition
2. an example
3. a historical fact

Pre-writing Tasks
Choose a Topic

A page 93
Answers will vary.

B Pair Work page 93
Answers will vary.

Organize Your Ideas

A page 94
Answers will vary.

B Pair Work page 94
Answers will vary.

Writing Task page 95
Answers will vary.

Peer Review

A page 95
Answers will vary.

B page 95
Answers will vary.

7 Comparison and Contrast 3
Family Values in Different Cultures

1 Grammar in the Real World

A Before You Read page 96

Answers will vary; Possible answer: Family can mean the
immediate family, parents, and children, and it can also
mean the immediate family plus extended family.

B Comprehension Check page 97

Possible answers:
1. His beliefs influenced how American families see their
   children.
2. Young Latino adults might live with their parents after
   college. Young American adults may live on their own.
3. The writer means that these ideas may not apply to
   everyone in Latino and U.S. cultures. The writer avoids
   stereotypes in this essay.

C Notice

1 Cause and Effect Writing page 97

U.S. Families' Characteristics	Latino Families' Characteristics
family = parents and children (immediate)	family = parents, children, aunts, uncles, etc. (extended)
family members = independent	family members = obligated to help each other
children = live away from their family when they become older	children = live with their parents when they become older

The writer used the block method.

2 Grammar page 98

1. In Dr. Spock's view, children should become more independent. The forms of the adjectives are different because of the length of the words. "Old" is a short adjective, so the comparative form is *-er*. "Independent" is a long adjective, so the comparative form is *more* + adjective.
2. The writer compares length of visits from relatives and the practice of young adults living with their parents until, and sometimes after, marriage.
3. They are the same in the importance of family.; "Despite these differences, U.S. culture <u>is similar to</u> Latino culture in terms of the importance of family." (lines 29–30); Families in both cultures do not behave the same; "Not all Latino families stick together. <u>Similarly</u>, not all U.S. parents point to the door when their children turn 18." (lines 32–33)

3 The Writing Process page 98

1. F
2. T
3. F
4. T
5. T

2 Comparative and Superlative Adjectives and Adverbs

Exercise 2.1 Comparative Adjectives and Adverbs

A pages 100–101

2. less likely than
3. less strictly than
4. more politely
5. less common
6. more involved than
7. less complex than

B Pair Work page 101

Answers will vary.

Exercise 2.2 Superlative Adjectives and Adverbs pages 101–102

2. the most important; *Answers will vary.*
3. strangest; *Answers will vary.*
4. the most difficult; *Answers will vary; Answers will vary.*
5. most significantly; *Answers will vary; Answers will vary.*
6. the hardest; *Answers will vary.*
7. the most patiently; *Answers will vary.*

Exercise 2.3 Comparative and Superlative Adjectives and Adverbs

A page 102

	High-Context	Low-Context	Collectivist	Individualist
2.	✓			
3.	✓			
4.		✓		
5.	✓			
6.			✓	
7.			✓	
8.			✓	
9.				✓
10.				✓

B page 103

2. less direct than
3. more directly
4. the most essential
5. more important
6. the biggest
7. more highly than
8. more valued than
9. less important than
10. the most critically

3 Articles

Exercise 3.1 Indefinite and Definite Articles

A pages 105–106

2. the
3. ∅
4. ∅
5. the
6. ∅
7. ∅
8. a
9. the
10. the
11. the
12. a
13. the
14. a/the
15. a
16. the
17. the

B Group Work page 106

Answers will vary.

Exercise 3.2 More Indefinite and Definite Articles

A pages 106–107

Answers will vary.

B Pair Work page 107

Answers will vary.

4 Common Expressions That Show Similarity

Exercise 4.1 Words That Show Similarity

A page 108

2. in common
3. similarities between
4. Like
5. is similar to
6. Similarly

B Pair Work page 108

Answers will vary.

5 Avoid Common Mistakes

Editing Task page 109

    The celebration of the New Year in South Korea is
not ^*the* same as in the United States. First of all, South Koreans
celebrate the Lunar New Year (the second new moon in
winter), so the date is not ^*the* same as in the United States,
where the New Year is celebrated on the first day of the
Gregorian Calendar (January 1). The New Year is ~~more~~
later in South Korea, usually in February. In addition, the
South Korean New Year celebration lasts for three days
and involves the entire family. According to ~~the~~ Dr. Sook-
Bin Woo, this is because South Korean families tend to be
~~more~~ closer than U.S. families. For example, South Korean
families play special games with each other during this
holiday. This family closeness may be the reason that many
South Koreans report that their ~~most~~ *best* childhood memories
are of New Year's celebrations.

    In the United States, the celebration of the New Year
begins on the evening of the last day of the year and
continues into the following day; it is therefore ~~more~~
shorter than the South Korean celebration. Traditionally,
it tends to be primarily an adult celebration for many
people. On New Year's Eve, many adults hire a babysitter
for their children and go out to a restaurant or to a party to
celebrate with other adults. Because U.S. celebrations often
do not include children, most Americans are unlikely to say
that their ~~most~~ *best* childhood memories are of the celebration

of the New Year. Sociologist ~~the~~ Dr. George Lee notes that
this tradition is changing in the United States as more
adults stay home and celebrate with their children.

6 The Writing Process
About Summarizing

Exercise

A page 111
Answers will vary.

B page 111
Answers will vary.

Pre-writing Tasks
Choose a Topic

A page 111
Answers will vary.

B Pair Work page 111
Answers will vary.

Organize Your Ideas

A page 112
Answers will vary.

B page 112
Answers will vary.

Writing Task page 113
Answers will vary.

Peer Review

A page 113
Answers will vary.

B page 113
Answers will vary.

8 Comparison and Contrast 4
Intercultural Communication

1 Grammar in the Real World

A Before You Read page 114
Answers will vary; Possible answer: Perception of time and
the amount of emotion expressed at a meeting are two
assumptions that may cause misunderstandings.

B Comprehension Check page 115

Possible answers:

1. The perceptions of time, the amount of emotion expressed during business interactions, and local customs are three main problems that business people might have.
2. Because they may see it as a way for people to influence a decision.
3. *Answers will vary.*

C Notice

1 Comparison and Contrast Writing page 115

Body Paragraph 1: Time in different cultures
1. <u>The United States and Germany – schedules and agendas are very important</u>
2. Mexico and Brazil – schedules and agendas not so important

Body Paragraph 2: Amount of emotions expressed
1. Parts of Italy – express feelings more openly
2. <u>Sweden – emotions are not as readily shown</u>

Body Paragraph 3: Local customs
1. Common practice in many business cultures
2. <u>Other cultures may see gift giving as a bribe</u>

2 Grammar page 116

1. *In contrast* can only come at the beginning of a sentence. *In contrast* is followed by a comma.
2. *Whereas* is similar to *while*.
3. *Even though* is similar to *while*, and *however* is similar to *in contrast*.
4. *Even though* is more appropriate because it conveys the surprise and unexpected contrast between something being appropriate in one culture and very inappropriate in another. *While* shows a general contrast.

3 The Writing Process page 116

1. ✓   4. ✓
2. ✓   5. _____
3. _____

2 Adverb Clauses of Contrast and Concession

Exercise 2.1 Adverb Clauses of Contrast

A page 117

	Most North Americans	Most Mexicans
2.		✓
3.	✓	
4.		✓
5.	✓	
6.	✓	
7.		✓

B page 118

Possible answers:

2. Whereas in Mexico, it is acceptable to arrive late to a meeting, especially to take care of personal business, in North America it is accepted that people will arrive on time.
3. In North America it's polite to arrive on time to a dinner party, whereas in Mexico, people tend to arrive late.
4. In Mexico, businesspeople generally share personal information at meetings, while North Americans tend to be more businesslike.
5. While in North America, people tend to call each other by their first names after they meet, in Mexico, people tend to be more formal.
6. In North America, people tend to have a direct communication style, while in Mexico, people tend to have a less direct communication style.
7. Whereas in Mexico people might not tell you immediately when they cannot attend an event, in North America people will tend to tell you immediately.

C Pair Work page 118

Answers will vary.

Exercise 2.2 Adverb Clauses of Concession

A pages 118–119

2. Though rank is important, gender bias is not common.
3. While the Chinese do not gesture or show much body language, this lack of gesturing does not mean a lack of responsiveness.
4. Although it is important to send written information about your company well before your arrival in China, Chinese businesspeople like to meet face-to-face rather than over the phone or by e-mail.
5. Even though Chinese business meetings are very formal affairs, the meetings may frequently be interrupted by the ringing of cell phones. *OR* Chinese business meetings are very formal affairs even though the meetings may frequently be interrupted by the ringing of cell phones.
6. Though Chinese businesspeople are hardworking and serious, they show a great sense of humor.
7. Although some companies may be very successful in their own countries, their success in China depends on a solid understanding of Chinese culture.

B Group Work page 119

Answers will vary.

3 Transition Words and Phrases That Show Contrast and Concession

Exercise 3.1 Transition Words and Prepositions That Show Contrast and Concession pages 121–122

2. In contrast,
3. Instead,
4. Despite
5. Nonetheless,
6. On the other hand,
7. On the contrary,
8. In spite of

Exercise 3.2 More Transition Words and Phrases and Prepositions That Show Contrast and Concession

Group Work page 122

Answers will vary.

4 Avoid Common Mistakes

Editing Task pages 123–124

Although the use of corporate websites is universal, ~~but~~ corporate website design is another aspect of doing business that differs from culture to culture. The different website designs for Good Foods are one example. The company operates globally. It wants to appear as though it sells the same quality products everywhere in the world. On ~~another~~ *the other* hand, the company wants to appeal to the consumers in each country where it does business. Therefore, the look of its sites differs from country to country. For example, the websites for Good Foods in the United States tend to use a limited number of colors. In contrast, the company site in India tends to use a great deal of color. The Indian version uses bright colors, such as pink, red, orange, and purple, while the U.S. version of the site uses only shades of blue and gray. This is because the way people interpret colors is cultural. Bright colors suggest "fun" to people in the United States, while blue and gray suggest "importance." In another example, the Good Foods site in Switzerland shows the company's products; however, it rarely shows people using or enjoying them. ~~In~~ *On* the other hand, when it does show people, they are usually alone. In contrast, the Good Foods site for Mexico shows families shopping together and large groups of people enjoying the products. This is because people in Mexico tend to prefer being with others. However, people in Switzerland value independence and solitude. Although the main purpose of a company's website is to present important information about the business, ~~but~~ the site must also address the cultural values of the people who view it.

5 The Writing Process
About Conclusions

Exercise

A Pair Work page 125

Answers will vary.

B page 125

Answers will vary.

Pre-writing Tasks

Choose a Topic

A page 126

Answers will vary.

B Pair Work page 126

Answers will vary.

Organize Your Ideas

A page 126

Answers will vary.

B Pair Work page 126

Answers will vary.

Writing Task pages 126–127

Answers will vary.

Peer Review

A page 127

Answers will vary.

B page 127

Answers will vary.

9 Narrative 1
The American Dream

1 Grammar in the Real World

A Before You Read page 128

Answers will vary; Possible answer: People are not as confident as they used to be about reaching the American Dream because of the changes in housing costs, job security, and the economy.

B Comprehension Check page 129

Possible answers:

1. The story of the three doctors is remarkable because the men were able to go to college and become doctors despite the fact that they grew up poor.
2. In the late 1980s and early 1990s, the costs of housing increased. Job security has become much less certain

since the late 1980s and early 1990s. The Great Recession in 2008 had a negative effect, too.

3. It holds Americans together and reassures them that the factors for success – ability, strong work ethic, and education – will be rewarded.

C Notice

1 Narrative Writing page 129

Possible answer: The writer chose this narrative to make a connection with the reader, and to provide real life examples to illustrate the topic.

2 Grammar page 129

1. (a) came first. The writer uses the past perfect to tell which event came first in the past.
2. (b) came first. The writer uses the past perfect.

3 The Writing Process page 130

Possible answers:

1. We treat them in hospitals every day. (line 1); The short sentence creates a serious and dramatic tone.
2. Two of us landed in juvenile-detention centers before our eighteenth birthdays.
   We knew we'd never survive if we went after it alone. But inspired early by caring and imaginative role models, one of us in childhood latched on to a dream of becoming a dentist, steered clear of trouble, and in his senior year of high school persuaded his two best friends to apply to a college program for minority students interested in becoming doctors.
3. However, when we . . .
   In addition, we are reminded . . .
   Nevertheless/However, inspired early by . . .
   Thus / As a result, we made a pact . . .

2 Past Perfect and Past Perfect Progressive

Exercise 2.1 Simple Past and Past Perfect

A page 132

2. arrived; had never been
3. stayed; had neglected
4. were; hadn't/had not found
5. contacted; had helped
6. were; had gone
7. had hoped; was
8. gave; had assisted

B Pair Work page 132

Answers will vary.

Exercise 2.2 Past Perfect and Past Perfect Progressive

A pages 132–133

2. had gone; had wanted / had been wanting
3. had lost; had been looking
4. had been thinking; had just started
5. had been worrying
6. had had; had hoped / had been hoping

B Pair Work page 133

Answers will vary.

3 Past Modals and Modal-like Expressions

Exercise 3.1 Past Modals and Modal-like Expressions page 135

2. didn't/did not have to drive
3. could/might have won
4. should/could have applied
5. didn't/did not have to go
6. could/might have been
7. couldn't/could not get
8. could buy
9. shouldn't/should not have loaned
10. could have predicted
11. couldn't/could not have guessed

Exercise 3.2 *Used To* and *Would*

A page 136

2. T	6. F
3. F	7. T
4. T	8. F
5. F	

B Pair Work page 136

Answers will vary.

Exercise 3.3 *Was / Were Supposed To* and *Was / Were Going To*

A pages 136–137

2. John was supposed/going to major in biology, but he changed his mind and decided to major in business instead.
3. John and his friends were supposed/going to go into business together after college, but they didn't have enough money.
4. John was supposed/going to move to California to find a job, but he was offered a job in Japan.
5. John was supposed/going to marry his high school sweetheart, but he fell in love with a girl in Japan.

6. John's parents were supposed/going to visit him this month, but his father broke his leg, so they postponed the trip.

B Pair Work page 137

Answers will vary.

4 Common Time Clauses

Exercise 4.1 Common Time Clauses

pages 138–139

2. He was two years old when his father left. *OR* When his father left, he was two years old.
3. After his father left, his mother struggled to take care of him and his brother. *OR* His mother struggled to take care of him and his brother after his father left.
4. When he was 12, he became interested in writing horror stories. *OR* He became interested in writing horror stories when he was 12.
5. While he was in school, he wrote many stories. *OR* He wrote many stories while he was in school.
6. He sold stories to his classmates until the teachers asked him to stop. *OR* Until the teachers asked him to stop, he sold stories to his classmates.
7. His first short story was published before he graduated college. *OR* Before he graduated college, his first short story was published.
8. After his mother died, his first novel, *Carrie*, was published. *OR* His first novel, *Carrie*, was published after his mother died.

Exercise 4.2 More Common Time Clauses

A pages 139–140

2. until   6. after
3. As   7. Since
4. After   8. As
5. Once

B page 140

Answers will vary.

5 Avoid Common Mistakes

Editing Task page 141

Jessica had always loved photography, even as a child.
      had been asking
She ~~was asking~~ for a camera for a long time when her
            given
father had ~~gave~~ her one on her tenth birthday. She would

take her camera everywhere and record the small moments

of everyday life that caught her eye: a cluster of leaves on

the sidewalk, or a spider web on a garden fence. Jessica
          seen
had always ~~see~~ photography as a hobby. Moreover, since

            come
she had ~~came~~ from a family that had endured economic
                                          known
hardships when she was growing up, she had always ~~know~~

that she had to choose a career that paid well and was

secure. Therefore, after high school, she got a degree in
                had been
landscape design. She ~~was~~ considering a job with the city

during her last year of college, but when her uncle, the

owner of a landscape company, asked her to work for him,
                          joined
she changed her mind. She ~~had joined~~ his landscaping

business right after graduation. However, Jessica never

lost her love of photography. She eventually bought herself

a higher quality camera and continued to take pictures

whenever she had the opportunity.
        had been
Jessica ~~was~~ working at the landscaping company

for about two years when her uncle decided to build a

website to advertise the business. He needed images

of the company's best work to publish on the site and
                                  had been
immediately thought of Jessica. She ~~was~~ taking photos of

the company's projects the entire time that she had worked
            was
there. The website ~~had been~~ a success. More importantly,

other companies saw it and wanted to know who the great

photographer was. Soon, Jessica was working full-time as

a photographer. Her uncle missed Jessica's presence, but

everyone was pleased that she was now earning a living

doing something that she truly loved.

6 The Writing Process

About Sentence Variety

Exercise

A page 143

Possible answers:

1. Being so full of food and nervous, it wasn't surprising that I couldn't fall asleep.
2. The next morning, due to oversleeping, I had to move very fast to get to the interview on time. *OR* When I finally fell asleep, my alarm clock turned off due to a power outage.
3. Since I hadn't had time to eat breakfast, I arrived at the interview very hungry.
4. I ran from the office covering my mouth. I learned a valuable lesson about job interviews. Never eat anything.

B Pair Work page 144

Answers will vary.

Pre-writing Tasks

Choose a Topic

A page 144

Answers will vary.

B Pair Work page 144

Answers will vary.

Organize Your Ideas

A page 144

Answers will vary.

B Pair Work page 144

Answers will vary.

Writing Task page 144

Answers will vary.

Peer Review

A page 145

Answers will vary.

B page 145

Answers will vary.

10 Narrative 2

Immigration

1 Grammar in the Real World

A Before You Read page 146

Answers will vary; Possible answer: Immigrants have contributed to the growth of many industries in the United States and helped turn it into one of the world's most powerful countries.

B Comprehension Check page 147

Possible answers:
1. These immigrants, called settlers, came from places like France and the Netherlands and most became farmers. This group of immigrants was small.
2. The government passed laws in 1921 restricting the number of immigrants coming to the United States. One reason was that people were troubled by the new religions and customs that immigrants brought.
3. Because the writer feels that immigrants will continue to settle in the United States and become part of its workforce and help its economy.

C Notice

1 Narrative Writing page 147

1600s: First wave of immigrants begins
1820s: Second wave of immigrants
1820s–1880s: Flood of immigrants
1921: 1921 immigration laws
2010s: Immigration debates

2 Grammar page 147

1. "These" refers to the particular immigrants who came during the 1820s to 1880s.
2. "That" refers to the time period from the 1890s to the beginning of the twentieth century.
3. . . . <u>from</u> the seventeenth century <u>through</u> the early nineteenth century . . . (line 6)
   <u>From</u> the 1820s <u>to</u> 1880s . . . (lines 9–10)

3 The Writing Process page 147

1. a, b
2. a, c

2 Demonstratives
Exercise 2.1 Demonstratives

A page 149

2. These/Those
3. This
4. This
5. These
6. This

B Pair Work page 149

Answers will vary.

Exercise 2.2 More Demonstratives

A page 150

2. fact
3. controversial issue
4. questionable claim
5. approach
6. people
7. argument

B Pair Work page 150

Answers will vary.

3 Common Time Signals
Exercise 3.1 Time Signals page 152

2. For six years
3. Every time
4. for many years
5. Over the next few years
6. after graduating high school
7. a few years later
8. now
9. every day
10. years ago
11. Years later
12. the first time

13. Now every morning
14. Over the next 20 years

Exercise 3.2 More Time Signals

A page 153

Answers will vary.

B Pair Work page 153

Answers will vary.

4 Avoid Common Mistakes

Editing Task page 154

The lack of clean drinking water is a problem in many parts of the world, but even when people have a source of water, collecting it can be arduous. Every morning, Isha gets water for her family. ~~Always it~~ *It always* takes her 30 minutes to get to the well and about an hour to walk back with a heavy clay container of water balanced on top of her head. By *the* time she returns, her body is aching from the weight of the water. She has been bringing water home like this for *the* last 20 years. Isha lives in Niger, a country in West Africa. In Africa, women, and sometimes children, ~~often~~ are *often* the ones responsible for collecting their family's water, and ~~these~~ *this* responsibility takes a toll on their bodies. For some women, the journey to a water source is very long. ~~This~~ *These* women have to walk up to 18 miles (30 kilometers) a day for water. Hans Hendrikse, a native South African, wanted to do something about this problem. Working with his engineer brother, Pieter, he created a new way of transporting water. It is called the Q-Drum. The Q-Drum is lightweight, durable, and affordable, and it can hold 50 liters of water. While ~~this~~ *these* features alone make the product appealing, the most groundbreaking feature is its doughnut shape. When a rope is looped through the hole in the Q-Drum, the container can be rolled along the ground like a wheel. The Q-Drum's unique design allows even a young child to pull water for several miles, so the women ~~never~~ will *never* have to carry the water solely on their heads. Over *the* next

decade this invention will have a major impact on the lives of the people of Africa, especially the women.

5 The Writing Process
About Audience and Purpose

Exercise

A pages 155–156

Text 1: 3
Text 2: 2
Text 3: 1
Text 4: 4

B Pair Work page 156

Answers will vary.

Pre-writing Tasks

Choose a Topic

A page 156

Answers will vary.

B Pair Work page 156

Answers will vary.

Organize Your Ideas

A page 156

Answers will vary.

B Group Work page 156

Answers will vary.

Writing Task page 157

Answers will vary.

Peer Review

A page 157

Answers will vary.

B page 157

Answers will vary.

11 Classification and Definition 1
Job Interviews

1 Grammar in the Real World

A Before You Read page 158

Answers will vary; Possible answer: Interviews are classified by their geographical location and format.

B Comprehension Check page 159

Possible answers:

1. Remote interviews are when the interviewer and interviewee are geographically separated. These are typically done during a first screening. Face-to-face interviews are done in person. They are normally done after the first round of remote screening.
2. An audition is less conventional because candidates are asked to perform a task that simulates what they will do on the job itself.
3. *Answers will vary.*

C Notice

1 Classification and Definition Writing page 159

Possible answers:

1. Remote interviews are conducted over the phone and used when candidates are geographically separated from the interviewers. They are the preferred method for initial screening.
2. Face-to-face interviews require the physical presence of the candidates. They are normally reserved for candidates who have already gone through a first round of remote screening.
3. Collective interviews have two structures: team interviews and group interviews.
4. Sequential interviews involve private one-on-one conversations between the candidate and one interviewer, one after another.
5. Structured interviews have a strict format. The same list of questions is rigidly followed with all candidates.
6. Unstructured interviews have a less strict format; candidates might be asked more open-ended questions that encourage them to lead the discussion.

2 Grammar page 159

1. lines 6–7
2. lines 13–14
3. lines 16–17
4. lines 30–32

The writer uses the passive. The passive focuses the reader on important terms like "interviews" and "multiple candidates." The subjects of the sentences aren't as important.

3 The Writing Process page 160

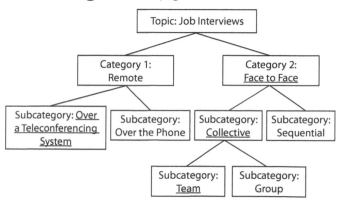

2 The Passive

Exercise 2.1 The Passive pages 162–163

2. You may not even be considered for the job if you arrive late to the interview.
3. During the interview, you will be asked questions about your résumé.
4. Interviews may be conducted over the phone.
5. One question you could ask is "What training programs are offered?"
6. The decision to employ someone is often based on a person's behavior during an interview.
7. Employers are prohibited by federal and state laws from asking certain questions about race, religion, and age.
8. Some employers have been known to give tests during interviews.
9. If you do well, you might be asked to come in for a second interview.
10. Interviewers often see more than one candidate in a day, so you will probably be compared with other candidates.

Exercise 2.2 More on the Passive

A page 163

2. were followed	7. can be learned
3. were asked	8. were given
4. were divided	9. had been told *OR* were told
5. was given	11. should be evaluated
6. were based	12. will be chosen

B Pair Work page 164

Answers will vary.

3 Common Words and Phrases Used in Classification Writing

Exercise 3.1 Classification Words and Phrases pages 165–166

2. c	6. b
3. a	7. c
4. c	8. a
5. a	

Exercise 3.2 More Classification Words and Phrases page 166

Possible answers:

2. The institutions are classified according to the types of degrees available and the fields of study or programs that are offered.
3. A university is generally composed of three programs: undergraduate, graduate, and professional.
4. Schools can be divided by their funding sources.
5. There are two funding classifications of schools, which are publicly supported schools and private schools.

6. Publicly supported schools can be subdivided into three groups: two-year community colleges, state universities, and state colleges.
7. There are many advantages of attending a community college, including lower tuition and smaller class sizes.

Exercise 3.3 More Classification Words and Phrases

A page 167

Answers will vary.

B Pair Work page 167

Answers will vary.

4 Avoid Common Mistakes

Editing Task page 168

There are many issues involved ~~on~~ *in* choosing an institution of higher education. A prospective student's choice might be based ~~in~~ *on* the location of the institution, or it might be based ~~in~~ *on* the reputation of the academic programs and the faculty. However, for many students, the process of choosing a university may *often* be ~~often~~ determined by economics. A college education may be one of the greatest expenditures an individual will make in his or her lifetime. If money is an issue in a student's choice, there are several funding options.

One funding option available to low-income college students is a grant. A grant is a sum of money that does not have to be paid back. Government programs are the primary source of education grants. In addition to government sources, grants may *sometimes* be ~~sometimes~~ awarded by private organizations and companies. The main factor involved ~~on~~ *in* the awarding of government grants is income level. Private grants may often be based ~~in~~ *on* additional factors such as ethnicity, grades, or other academic achievements. As reporting one's income is always involved ~~on~~ *in* the process of applying for a grant, a good place to begin is with the U.S. Department of Education's Free Application for Federal Student Aid (FAFSA). The FAFSA application

simplifies the income reporting process and matches the applicant's income with several grant opportunities. Grants are often the first and best choice for students who cannot afford a college education on their own.

5 The Writing Process
About Classifying

Exercise

A page 169

1. c
2. a
3. b

B Pair Work page 169

Answers will vary.

Pre-writing Tasks

Choose a Topic

A page 170

Answers will vary.

B Pair Work page 170

Answers will vary.

Organize Your Ideas

A page 170

Answers will vary.

B Pair Work page 170

Answers will vary.

Writing Task pages 170–171

Answers will vary.

Peer Review

A page 171

Answers will vary.

B page 171

Answers will vary.

12 Classification and Definition 2
Your Ideal Job

1 Grammar in the Real World

A Before You Read page 172

Answers will vary; The six personality types are Artistic, Investigative, Realistic, Social, Enterprising, and Conventional.

B Comprehension Check page 173

Possible answers:

1. People's career choices are so important for success because work is an enormous part of people's lives.
2. It can help people in choosing satisfying jobs and careers.
3. *Answers will vary.*

C Notice

1 Classification and Definition Writing page 174

Personality type	Definition
1. Social	A person who has good skills at teaching, counseling, nursing, or giving information.
2. Enterprising	A person who is good at leading people or selling things.
3. Realistic	A person who values environments where they produce goods or use machines.

2 Grammar page 174

1. An Artistic personality type <u>refers to</u> a person who enjoys creative activities like art, dance, or creative writing, and who generally avoids highly structured or repetitive activities.
2. A person with an Investigative personality type, on the other hand, <u>is defined as</u> someone who likes to study and solve math or science problems.
3. Having a Realistic personality type <u>means</u> valuing practical work, such as jobs that require technical or manual skills and are productive.
4. They <u>are referred to as</u> Social personalities.

3 The Writing Process page 174

1. "Their" refers to people.
2. values
3. The writer uses the words "match" and "suit" to strengthen the connection between the sentences.

2 The Language of Definition

Exercise 2.1 Identifying the Parts of Definitions

A page 176

2. An architect is a person who designs new buildings and makes certain that they are built correctly.
3. People who work in stores and sell merchandise are sometimes referred to as sales associates.
4. Someone who is skilled in playing music is called a musician.
5. Sculptors are artists who make art out of materials like clay, marble, and metal.
6. People who help their clients choose fashionable clothing, hairstyles, and makeup are known as stylists.

B page 177

2. A person who designs new buildings and makes certain that they are built correctly is referred to as an architect.
3. Sales associates are people who work in stores and sell merchandise.
4. A musician is defined as someone who is skilled in playing music.
5. Artists who make art out of materials like clay, marble, and metal are known as sculptors.
6. Stylists are people who help their clients choose fashionable clothing, hairstyles, and makeup.

C Pair Work page 177

Answers will vary.

Exercise 2.2 Writing Definitions

A page 177

2. law
3. testimony
4. to appeal
5. to sentence
6. bankruptcy

B page 178

2. Law is a system or rules that a community recognizes as regulators of behaviors and actions of people. *OR* A system or rules that a community recognizes as regulators of behaviors and actions of people is law.
3. Evidence presented orally by witnesses during trials or before grand juries is known as testimony.
4. To appeal means to ask a higher court to review a decision after a trial to determine if it was correct.
5. To give punishment to someone convicted of a crime is called "to sentence."
6. A legal procedure for dealing with the debt problems of individuals and businesses is referred to as bankruptcy.

3 Appositives

Exercise 3.1 Appositives pages 180–181

2. Steve Jobs, a driving force in technology, had an enormous impact on the way we use technology on a daily basis.
3. One supporter of the non-profit housing organization Habitat for Humanity is Jimmy Carter, a former U.S. president.
4. Desmond Tutu, a Nobel Peace Prize laureate and retired South African Archbishop, has promoted peaceful conflict resolution for many years.
5. Dr. Douglas Schwartzentruber and Dr. Larry Kwak, cancer researchers, are both working separately to find a vaccine against cancer.
6. Bono, a famous singer with the band U2, works to improve health and nutrition throughout the world.
7. Howard Gardner proposed nine types of intelligences (Table 1).
8. The Ronald McDonald House Charities (RMHC) helps families of children who are receiving medical treatment for serious diseases.

Answers will vary.

4 Avoid Common Mistakes

Editing Task page 182

The Myers-Briggs Type Indicator, MBTI, is a personality
assessment tool ~~who~~ *that* has increasingly gained popularity
in the workplace. It is based on a psychological theory
developed by Carl Jung. Jung proposed that there are
two basic categories of thinking styles: rational and
irrational. Rational functions involve thinking and
feeling. Irrational functions involve sensing and intuition.
Jung further proposed that there are two basic types of
people, introverts and extroverts. While there are several
personality qualities ~~who~~ *that* psychologists associate with each
type, introverts are usually ~~define~~ *defined* as people who are more
interested in ideas and thinking. In contrast, extroverts are
~~define~~ *defined* as people who are more action-oriented. The MBTI
has taken these four basic Jungian personality categories
and types and established four sets of opposing pairs:
extrovert/introvert, sensing/intuition, thinking/feeling,
and judgment/perception. While individuals use all of
these thinking styles, their MBTI results indicate their
thinking-style preferences. They can help match individuals
to careers and help managers understand how to best work
with these employees.

One of the MBTI personality types, ISTJ (Introvert,
Sensing, Thinking, Judgment), illustrates the way in
which the MBTI assessment tool can match individuals
to appropriate working environments. ISTJ personality
types are ~~a person~~ *people* who ~~tends~~ *tend* to be quiet. They prefer to
be alone. They attend to details rather than to the Big
Picture. They prefer thinking to feeling. This means that
they use logic when making decisions. ISTJ personality
types like controlled, organized environments. They are

concrete, ordered, and predictable. They are more in tune
with facts than with other people's feelings. ISTJs do well
as accountants and in law enforcement. Managers of ISJT
types who are having difficulty getting along with others
need to take action. ~~They~~ *ISTJs* can be placed in situations
where they can work alone, for example. Other remedies
for unhappy ISTJs might include moving them to a more
organized work group.

5 The Writing Process
About Cohesive Devices

Exercise page 183

2. 6	5. 5
3. 2	6. 1
4. 3	7. 3

Pre-writing Tasks

Choose a Topic

A page 184

Answers will vary.

B Pair Work page 185

Answers will vary.

C Pair Work page 185

Answers will vary.

Organize Your Ideas

A page 185

Answers will vary.

B Pair Work page 186

Answers will vary.

Writing Task page 186

Answers will vary.

Peer Review

A page 187

Answers will vary.

B page 187

Answers will vary.

13 Problem–Solution 1
Food and Technology

1 Grammar in the Real World

A Before You Read page 188

Answers will vary; Possible answer: The writer wants to see labels that show the presence of GM foods.

B Comprehension Check page 189

Possible answers:

1. GM foods are found in 60 to 70 percent of the foods in American supermarkets, yet there has been little research on the short-term and long-term effects of GM foods on our health.
2. It can improve the nutritional value or protect food from pests.
3. There has been little research to back the claims that genetically modified foods are really "enhanced," or better for you. They may actually be dangerous.

C Notice

1 Problem–Solution Writing page 189

Possible answers:

Source	Information
The Center for Food Safety	GM foods have entered nearly every sector of the food market. A majority of the public is consuming GM foods as part of their regular diet.
Patrick Byrne	From 60 to 70 percent of all prepared foods in a typical supermarket in the United States contain GM ingredients.
Larry Trivieri	The U.S. Food and Drug Administration does not require independent safety tests on GM foods.
Neal Barnard	Potential health risks may be associated with the consumption of GM foods.

2 Grammar page 190

1. a. a period of time up to now
   b. the action is probably continuing; the present perfect progressive form emphasizes that the action is probably continuing
2. The statistics are connected to a specific time in the past.

3 The Writing Process page 190

1. strong opinion
2. fact
3. statistic
4. emotional appeal

2 Present Perfect and Present Perfect Progressive

Exercise 2.1 Present Perfect Forms or Simple Past?

A page 192

2. have gotten / have been getting

3. was
4. started
5. 've/have always applied
6. 've/have sprayed
7. 've/have lived *OR* 've/have been living
8. have been used
9. used
10. didn't/did not work
11. stopped
12. went

B Pair Work page 193

Answers will vary.

Exercise 2.2 More Present Perfect Forms or Simple Past? page 193

2. (For the past 20 years,) researchers have been tracking the areas used to grow GM crops in the world.
3. (Over the past 15 years,) the number of GM crops has grown significantly.
4. Over 309 million acres of land were used for GM crops (in 2008) compared to 282 million in 2007.
5. Many people are not even aware that farmers began growing GM crops (in the mid-nineties).
6. Statistics show that the global area of GM crops has increased / has been increasing steadily (since the mid-nineties).
7. (In 2010,) farmers from 29 countries, including Brazil, Argentina, and India, planted GM crops.
8. The effects of GM foods on people have not been determined , and scientists (continue) to do research.
9. Research has not shown (yet) that GM foods have a negative effect on our health and environment.
10. (Until) there is definite proof that GM foods are not harmful, some people have decided to avoid them.

Exercise 2.3 More Present Perfect Forms and Simple Past page 194

2. T
3. F
4. T
5. T
6. T
7. T
8. F
9. T
10. T

3 Common Noun Phrase Structures

Exercise 3.1 Noun Phrases with *Of*

A page 196

2. the aims of
3. the effects of
4. the majority of; a number of
   OR a number of; the majority of
5. the heart of
6. The number of

7. the benefits of
8. the basis of

B Group Work page 196

Answers will vary.

Exercise 3.2 Noun Phrases with That Clauses

A page 197

2. The notion that
3. the fact that
4. possibility that

5. the view that
6. the hope that
7. the fact that

B Pair Work page 197

Answers will vary.

4 Avoid Common Mistakes

Editing Task page 198

    A number of animal rights ~~activist thinks~~ *activists think* that laboratory-generated meat, also known as cultured meat, provides a solution to the negative environmental effects of food production. Cultured meat is grown in a laboratory from animal tissue cells. There are many benefits of cultured meat. First, animals do not have to be killed for food. According to the animal rights organization People for the Ethical Treatment of Animals (PETA), "More than 40 billion chickens, fish, pigs, and cows are killed every year for food in the United States" (as cited in Harder, 2008, para. 1). ~~This~~ *The* fact that cultured meat would virtually eliminate animal suffering is not in dispute. Additionally, most people are aware that raising animals for food is harmful to the environment. This is because processing meat requires large amounts of resources such as land and water. There is also a great deal of ~~informations~~ *information* on ~~this~~ *the* fact that raising animals for meat contributes to greenhouse gases and pollutes water, air, and land. Recent ~~researches~~ *research* on the environmental impact of cultured meat is very promising. A number of ~~environmentalist agrees~~ *environmentalists agree* that cultured meat would greatly reduce greenhouse gas emissions. There is also ~~evidences~~ *evidence* that cultured meat might be healthier and safer. A number of ~~scientist is~~ *scientists are* continuing to do ~~researches~~ *research* on cultured meat.

Many of these experts predict that we will see cultured meat in supermarkets within five to ten years. It seems clear that relying more on engineered food products may someday help to solve some of the environmental problems that we face today.

5 The Writing Process
About Emphasizing the Significance of a Problem

Exercise

A page 200

Answers will vary.

B Pair Work page 200

Answers will vary.

Pre-writing Tasks

Choose a Topic

A page 200

Answers will vary.

B Pair Work page 200

Answers will vary.

Organize Your Ideas

A page 200

Answers will vary.

B Group Work page 201

Answers will vary.

Writing Task page 201

Answers will vary.

Peer Review

A page 201

Answers will vary.

B page 201

Answers will vary.

14 Problem–Solution 2
Children and Health

1 Grammar in the Real World

A Before You Read page 202

Answers will vary; Possible answer: The author identifies the main causes of childhood obesity as overworked parents who have no time to prepare healthy food, a lack of sidewalks and safe outside play areas for children, and the marketing of inexpensive large-portion meals at fast-food restaurants.

B Comprehension Check page 203

Possible answers:

1. Obese children and adolescents may be at a high risk for cardiovascular disease, asthma, sleep apnea, and Type 2 diabetes.
2. Some social consequences could be social discrimination, low self-esteem, and poor academic performance.
3. The reasons children are becoming obese are due to many factors, including societal issues. Therefore, there is no simple reason for the rise in childhood obesity.

C Notice

1 Problem–Solution Writing page 203

Reasons for the Problem:

1. overworked parents
2. lack of sidewalks and safe outside play areas
3. the marketing of inexpensive large portion meals at fast food restaurants

Consequences of the Problem:

1. high blood pressure
2. high cholesterol
3. asthma
4. Type 2 diabetes

2 Grammar page 204

2. asserts that
3. have indicated that
4. notes that
5. believe that

3 The Writing Process page 204

Homelife Patterns
- ~~unsupervised children, parents allow children too much freedom~~
- parents always at work, no time to fix healthy meals

Nutrition
- cheap fast food, young children want prizes
- ~~not enough vegetables and fruit~~
- ~~too much processed food~~
- ~~soda or high-sugar juices instead of water~~

Lack of Physical Activity
- ~~watching TV~~
- ~~playing computer games and handheld games~~
- less outdoor activity – no safe places

2 Reporting Verbs

Exercise 2.1 Reporting Verbs page 206

Dear Editor,

I want to bring your readers' attention to the issue of childhood obesity in the United States. Recent studies show that 32 percent of children and adolescents in the United States are overweight. Doctors claim that unhealthy

childhood weight can affect adult weight. Some reports estimate that children who are overweight before the age of 15 are 80 percent more likely to be obese at 25 than children with healthy weights.

Experts suggest that some of the main causes of childhood obesity are a lack of parental influences, a lack of nutritious foods available in the home, and availability of fast-food restaurants. However, we should also consider the role that school plays in influencing a child's diet and weight. Because students spend a large part of their day at school, that is where they do much of their eating. Research indicates that children get about 40 percent of their daily calories while they are at school. This statistic suggests a link between school lunches and childhood obesity. In addition, most students these days have to do a lot of homework. Some parents estimate that their children have to do more than three hours of homework a night. This keeps them from spending their after-school time engaging in physical activities. I don't want to blame schools for childhood obesity, but I do think we should all work together to help our children be healthy.

Sincerely,
A concerned parent

Exercise 2.2 More Reporting Verbs

A page 207

2. a. emphasizes that
3. b. believes that
4. a. states that
5. c. points out that
6. c. claims that
7. b. demonstrate that
8. b. has alleged that

B Pair Work page 207

Answers will vary.

Exercise 2.3 Using Reporting Verbs

Pair Work page 208

Answers will vary.

3 Adverb Clauses and Phrases with As

Exercise 3.1 Using Adverb Clauses with As

A page 209

2. As shown in/by Chart 1, nine percent of Virginia youth are obese. *OR* As Chart 1 shows, nine percent of Virginia youth are obese.
3. As illustrated in Chart 1, the majority of Virginia youth aren't/are not overweight. *OR* As Chart 1 illustrates, the majority of Virginia youth aren't/are not overweight.
4. As Chart 1 points out, most Virginia youth are active at least four days a week.

5. As demonstrated in/by Chart 1, 32 percent of Virginia youth aren't/are not at a healthy weight. OR As Chart 1 demonstrates, 32 percent of Virginia youth aren't/are not at a healthy weight.
6. As can/may be seen in Chart 2, 12 percent of Virginia youth are active less than two days per week.

B Pair Work page 209
Answers will vary.

Exercise 3.2 Using Adverb Phrases with *As* page 210
Possible answers:
2. As shown by Chart 3, the percentage of Virginia youth who don't watch TV is smaller than the percentage who don't play video/computer games.
3. As can be seen in Chart 3, the percentage of Virginia youth who spend one hour or less playing video/computer games is larger than the percentage who spend one hour or less watching TV.
4. As seen in Chart 3, the percentage of Virginia youth who spend three hours per day playing video/computer games is smaller than the percentage who play one hour per day.
5. As is seen in Chart 3, the percentage of Virginia youth who don't watch TV or play video/computer games is larger than the percentage who spend five or more hours watching TV or playing video/computer games.

4 Common Vocabulary for Describing Information in Graphics
Exercise 4.1 Vocabulary to Describe Chart Information

A page 212

Oct: low	Feb: high
Nov: low	Mar: high
Dec: moderate	Apr: high
Jan: very low	May: very high

B Pair Work page 212
Answers will vary.

Exercise 4.2 More Vocabulary to Describe Chart Information page 212
Answers will vary.

5 Avoid Common Mistakes
Editing Task page 213
Possible answers:

Several studies have shown ~~that~~ a connection between genetics and obesity. As ~~the~~ Smith's 2009 study shows, people who have access to exactly the same foods will use those calories differently. Figure A demonstrates ~~that~~ the differences. It shows how a controlled diet and exercise program affected a group of 50 participants: some people in the group gained weight, others maintained their weight, and a small percentage even lost weight. From this study, it can *be* inferred that these different responses to the same situation are primarily genetic. Wu's research (2009) provides further support for the genetic connection to obesity. Her 2010 long-range study on body weight and family history clearly demonstrates ~~that~~ a genetic link to obesity. As ~~the~~ Figure B illustrates, there was very little variation in body weight among three generations of ten families. Finally, several studies have shown ~~that~~ a connection between a gene called FTO and obesity. These studies also demonstrate ~~that~~ a relationship between FTO and diabetes and other diseases. From these and other studies, it can *be* argued that genetics plays a role in body weight.

6 The Writing Process
About Narrowing Down a Topic
Exercise
A Pair Work page 215
Answers will vary.

B Group Work page 215
Answers will vary.

Pre-writing Tasks
Choose a Topic
A page 215
Answers will vary.

B Pair Work page 215
Answers will vary.

Organize Your Ideas
A page 216
Answers will vary.

B Pair Work page 216
Answers will vary.

Writing Task pages 216–217
Answers will vary.

Peer Review

A page 217

Answers will vary.

B page 217

Answers will vary.

15 Problem–Solution 3
Health and Technology

1 Grammar in the Real World

A Before You Read page 218

Answers will vary; Possible answer: Doctors are concerned that patients are self-diagnosing, that they do not use credible websites, and that they will scare themselves when reading symptoms online.

B Comprehension Check page 219

1. Cyberchondria is when people with no medical background diagnose themselves by looking up information about their symptoms on the Internet. They often conclude that they have a worse condition than what their doctor has diagnosed.
2. Doctors are concerned that patients will scare themselves when reading about symptoms online because they don't have any context to go with the information they find online.
3. The solution has three parts: Health-care websites need to state that their information should be in addition to, and not a substitute for, consultation and treatment by a doctor; doctors need to realize that they are no longer the only source of information on medical conditions and should educate their patients on how to use the information they find on medical websites; and patients should check that the information they find online is up-to-date and credible before visiting a doctor.

C Notice

1 Problem–Solution Writing pages 219–220

1. Health-care websites must state clearly that their information should be used in addition to a consultation with a doctor and medical treatment.
2. Doctors should realize they are no longer the only source of medical information.
3. Doctors should educate their patients about how to evaluate the health information they find on the Internet.
4. Patients should remember that no website can replace a doctor's physical exam.
5. Patients should check that the information medical websites have is up-to-date and credible.

2 Grammar page 220

1. in order to solve this problem

2. the *-ing* (gerund) form; cyberchondria
3. "When searching . . ." doesn't have a subject and main verb. "However, when health-care website providers . . ." has a subject and main verb.

3 The Writing Process page 220

b) It summarizes the main parts of the solution.

2 Adverb Clauses of Purpose and Infinitives of Purpose

Exercise 2.1 Adverb Clauses and Infinitives of Purpose page 222

Before the invention of the Internet, people would visit their doctors <u>in order to find out what was wrong with them</u>. These days, when people begin to feel ill, they often turn to the Internet <u>to diagnose themselves</u>. Many medical professionals agree that self-diagnosis by the Internet can often cause unnecessary and unwarranted fears. However, once in a while, the patient's hunches are correct.

Take the case of Alison Chambers. Alison has a 10-year-old son named Miles. When Miles was about two years old, he began getting fevers on a regular basis. She took him to a doctor <u>to get help</u>, and her doctor told her that children often get fevers and it was nothing to worry about. The doctor told Alison that Miles should stay home from day care when other children were ill <u>so as not to get sick</u>. He also said that Miles should wash his hands often <u>so that he did not pick up other children's germs as readily</u>. Although Alison was very careful to follow the doctor's advice, Miles continued to get a fever about once a month. She took Miles to three more doctors <u>so that she could get other opinions</u>, but they all agreed with her doctor's diagnosis.

Alison began to get very frustrated and started researching Miles's symptoms online <u>so as to find out some information for herself</u>. She read about a rare disease whose symptoms sounded like Miles's symptoms. She visited Miles's doctor <u>to ask his opinion</u>. He thought it was unlikely that Miles had the disease, but he agreed to test him for it. The test showed that Miles did have the rare disease. Alison was scared but relieved to know what was wrong with her son. Miles received treatment and stopped getting fevers soon after. It can be dangerous to rely on the Internet for medical information, but in Alison and Miles's case, it paid off.

Exercise 2.2 More Adverb Clauses and Infinitives of Purpose

A page 223

Possible answers:
2. He needed a "cheering section" to hold himself responsible.
3. She uses it to give her data on the fat, calories, and protein in her meals.

4. She uses it to keep track of how long she runs and the calories she uses.
5. People need to commit so that the changes become long-term habits.
6. We need to arrive at the doctor's office armed with knowledge so as not to waste time in our discussions with doctors.
7. Doctor's will need to change their relationship with patients in order to keep up with them.
8. He wants her to tell listeners one last thing to inspire them to use digital technology to improve their health.

B Pair Work page 223

Answers will vary.

3 Reducing Adverb Clauses to Phrases

Exercise 3.1 Reducing Adverb Clauses

A page 225

2. After having visited a few sites,
3. While looking at the list,
4. When doing research,
5. when considering which websites to go to,
6. After having read an article that interests you,
7. when visiting websites that try to sell you products
8. After collecting all the information,
9. After being diagnosed,

B Pair Work page 225

Answers will vary.

Exercise 3.2 Adverb Phrases page 226

Possible answers:

2. While going through treatment, people find it comforting to communicate with others diagnosed with their disease.
3. After talking with others about their illness, people don't feel so alone.
4. Before choosing a group to join, people should read the messages that members post to make sure the group is supportive.
5. While monitoring members' messages, leaders should encourage positive participation.
6. When noticing that a member is going through a difficult time, the members of good groups offer encouragement and advice.
7. After receiving the support they asked for, members of good groups stay with the group and give others support.

4 Common Vocabulary to Describe Problems and Solutions

Exercise 4.1 Phrases to Introduce Problems and Solutions page 228

2. A secondary issue
3. One solution for the first problem
4. The problem of
5. can be solved by
6. While
7. are issues
8. the most urgent issue is
9. There are several ways to address the problem of
10. is necessary

Exercise 4.2 Phrases to Introduce Problems and Solutions

A Pair Work page 229

Answers will vary.

B Group Work page 229

Answers will vary.

5 Avoid Common Mistakes

Editing Task page 230

A solution to the problem of ~~the~~ cyberchondria is to help individuals become informed Internet users. The Internet can be a useful source of information, but only if people use it wisely. Individuals need to know how to evaluate search ~~results, so~~ *results so that* they can avoid misleading information. For ~~examples,~~ *example* a website may be out of date, or it may not be published by a credible medical source. Users should look for a date somewhere on the ~~site, so~~ *site so that* they know that content is updated regularly. The solution to the problem of ~~the~~ unreliable medical websites is to establish the validity of sites. For ~~examples,~~ *example* users should avoid sites with URLs ending in ".com" and sites that do not have scientific or medical sponsors. A commercial website that looks like a medical source may actually be a business selling products. However, medical sites with URLs ending in ".gov" or ".edu" tend to have credible ~~content so that~~ *content, so* users can be more confident of the information they contain. Physicians can also help solve the problem of ~~the~~ cyberchondria by

directing their patients to their own preferred sites. This
will reduce patient anxiety and ~~frustration, so~~ *frustration so that* physicians

can use their consultation time more productively.

6 The Writing Process
About Evaluating Proposed Solutions

Exercise

A page 231

2. d   4. a
3. b   5. c

B Pair Work page 232

2. *Answers will vary;* limitation type 1
3. *Answers will vary;* limitation type 3
4. *Answers will vary;* limitation type 2
5. *Answers will vary;* limitation type 4

Pre-writing Tasks

Choose a Topic

A page 232

Answers will vary.

B Pair Work page 232

Answers will vary.

Organize Your Ideas

A page 232

Answers will vary.

B Pair Work page 232

Answers will vary.

Writing Task page 233

Answers will vary.

Peer Review

A page 233

Answers will vary.

B page 233

Answers will vary.

16 Problem–Solution 4
Leading a Healthy Life

1 Grammar in the Real World

A Before You Read page 234

Answers will vary; Possible answer: Make a few small
changes in eating and exercise habits to improve health.

B Comprehension Check page 235

Possible answers:
1. Busy work schedules prevent them from exercising,
   getting enough sleep, and eating well.
2. When it comes to healthy eating and exercising, some
   people believe that these are difficult tasks that are very
   time-consuming.
3. *Answers will vary.*

C Notice

1 Problem–Solution Writing page 235

Proposed Solution 1:
Change eating habits

Steps:
1. Buy low-calorie and low-fat foods that are easy to cook.
2. <u>Cook more quantities of food over the weekend and
   freeze the leftovers.</u>

Proposed Solution 2:
<u>Incorporate exercise into everyday life</u>

Steps:
1. <u>Find an activity that is enjoyable.</u>
2. <u>Commit to that activity and make it part of your routine.</u>

2 Grammar pages 235–236

1. The *it* in "... it is not impossible ..." (lines 4–5) does not
   refer to a previous noun. The *it* in "... nor does it have
   to be time-consuming ..." (lines 11–12) refers to *living a
   healthy* life in the previous line.
2. The passive makes the sentence more objective.
3. The writer uses the adjective *essential.*

3 The Writing Process page 236

Background information: Paragraph 1
Description of the problem: Paragraph 2
Solution: Paragraphs 3–4
Steps of the solution: Paragraphs 3–4
Limitations of the solution: Paragraph 3 ("It has been
argued that freezing the food ...")
Conclusion: Paragraph 5

2 *It* Constructions
Exercise 2.1 *It* Constructions

A pages 239–240

2. c; It is easy for everyone to eat good food by planning
   meals ahead of time.
3. c; It is unusual for young people to pay attention to their
   dietary habits.
4. a; It is possible that meditation or yoga can
   reduce stress.
5. a; It is clear that doctors agree that people should focus
   on their exercise and eating habits.
6. b; It is indisputable that moderate exercise results in
   fewer diseases such as diabetes.
7. c; It might be true that working out regularly improves
   mood.

8. b; It is impossible to say why some people like to exercise and some don't.
9. a; It is unlikely that regular exercise can cause physical harm.
10. c; It is evident that good support systems have a positive impact on one's health.

B Pair Work page 240

Answers will vary.

Exercise 2.2 Passive It Constructions

A page 240

1. b. In the 60s, it was believed that tobacco was good for the body.
   c. Years ago, it was thought that cigarettes might lengthen a person's life and were good for his or her teeth.
2. a. It has been recently shown that sugar is bad for one's health.
   b. Years ago, it was argued that sugar was a good source of energy for children.
3. a. Now, it has generally been accepted that watching too much television is bad for children.
   b. It has been suggested that too much television keeps children from doing physical activities.
   c. In the 60s, it was believed that watching television could improve children's grades.

B Group Work page 241

Answers will vary.

3 Common Transition Words to Indicate Steps of a Solution
Exercise 3.1 Transition Words to Indicate Steps of a Solution

A page 242

2. Next, it's necessary to; which strategies will address them
3. Following that,; the strategies
4. Finally,; the effectiveness of the solutions after six months

B Pair Work page 242

Answers will vary.

Exercise 3.2 More Transition Words to Indicate Steps of a Solution page 243

2; 6; 1; 3; 4; 7; 8; 5

4 Avoid Common Mistakes

Editing Task page 244

It is ~~importand~~ *important* to get an adequate amount of sleep in order to maintain a healthy lifestyle. For many people, it is almost impossible ~~to~~ get a good night's sleep. Stress and the demands of work have a tremendous effect on one's ability to sleep. Lack of sleep can also result from certain lifestyle habits. However, it is virtually impossible ~~for~~ people to function well without adequate sleep. Studies have shown that lack of sleep can lead to a variety of physical and emotional problems. Therefore, it is ~~import~~ *important* to get at least seven to eight hours of sleep at night because getting the recommended amount of sleep means optimal health and energy, more acute mental faculties, and a better memory. It also means getting sick less and being better able to deal with the stresses and strains of everyday life. Although at times it may seem impossible ~~to~~ get enough sleep, there are a few simple strategies for improving one's chances. First, one needs to determine the causes of sleeplessness, such as lack of exercise or consuming too much caffeine. ~~Than~~ *Then*, one needs to commit to making a few small lifestyle changes. People who have difficulty sleeping should increase their daily exercise, but not exercise too late in the day. They should avoid consuming too much caffeine and eating close to bedtime. It is also ~~importand~~ *important* to have a regular bedtime and to get the same number of hours of sleep each night. These small changes to one's daily routine can lead to a better night's sleep and improved health.

5 The Writing Process
About Describing the Steps of a Solution

Exercise

A pages 245–246

1. Three
2. Yes: *First, Next, Finally*

3. Importance
4. First, parents and teachers should learn about the warning signs of eating disorders and other body-image issues. Next, they should think about how they compliment girls. Finally, they should give young people a place where they can talk openly about how they feel when comparing themselves to thin girls or models they may see in fashion magazines.

B Pair Work page 246

Answers will vary.

Pre-writing Tasks

Choose a Topic

A page 246

Answers will vary.

B Pair Work page 246

Answers will vary.

Organize Your Ideas

A page 246

Answers will vary.

B Pair Work page 246

Answers will vary.

Writing Task page 247

Answers will vary.

Peer Review

A page 247

Answers will vary.

B page 247

Answers will vary.

17 Summary–Response
Privacy in the Digital Age

1 Grammar in the Real World

A Before You Read page 248

Answers will vary; Possible answer: The writers suggest using privacy controls on social networking sites and going on websites that have security padlocks.

B Comprehension Check page 249

Possible answers:
1. The writer suggests that people use privacy controls on social networking sites and use only secure sites when purchasing products.

2. The summary-response writer believes that the issues concerning posting information on health issues, job dissatisfaction, and political views are missing.
3. *Answers will vary.*

C Notice

1 Summary–Response Writing page 250
1. According; to; Erani
2. As; the; author; points; out
3. The; author; further; states

2 Grammar page 250
1. The people who went on vacation had their homes broken into.; *If they had not posted those details, the thieves would not have known that they had gone away.*; The unreal conditional helps the writer support his point that sometimes personal information ends up in the hands of criminals.
2. The man who bought merchandise on a website that did not have a security padlock had his bank accounts emptied.; *If he had paid attention to the security on the site, he would not have lost his money.*; The unreal conditional helps the writer support his point that purchasing products on websites without security padlocks can be risky.
3. *While it may be impossible to entirely eliminate the risks, if people followed reasonable guidelines to protect important data, they could greatly reduce these risks.* (lines 26–28); The *if* clause in 2 refers to an imagined past result.; This *if* clause refers to an imagined present result.; The verbs in 2 are in the past perfect, the verbs in the 3 are in the simple past.

3 The Writing Process page 250
1. Para. 1 Lines 1 to 6   3. Para. 4 Lines 26 to 28
2. Para. 2 Lines 11 to 14

2 Past Unreal Conditionals
Exercise 2.1 Past Unreal Conditionals
pages 252–253

2. hadn't/had not been; would have shredded
3. had taken; would/could/might have had
4. had found; would/could/might have had
5. 'd/had realized; would/could/might have been
6. hadn't/had not stolen; wouldn't/would not have
7. hadn't/had not warned; could/might have had

Exercise 2.2 More Past Unreal Conditionals

A pages 253–253

Possible answers:
2. If Eric had been ready to go swimming on Saturday morning, I wouldn't have gone to the beach alone.
3. If Eric had been with me, I wouldn't have left my wallet and phone on the beach while I went swimming.

4. If I hadn't gone swimming, someone wouldn't have stolen my credit cards and my phone.
5. If I hadn't forgotten the address of Eric's house, I could have found the house.
6. If I had had my cell phone, I could have called Eric.
7. If my cell phone had been password-protected, the thief wouldn't have been able to use my phone.
8. If I hadn't had personal information on my cell phone, the thief wouldn't have gotten my bank account numbers.
9. If I hadn't forgotten to wear sunscreen, I wouldn't have a terrible sunburn.

B Pair Work page 254

Answers will vary.

3 Common Phrases Used in Summary–Response Writing

Exercise 3.1 Summarizing Information
page 256

2. starts the article
3. describes
4. notes that
5. goes on to explain
6. acknowledges that
7. argues that
8. according to the article,
9. concludes
10. does not mention at all

Exercise 3.2 More Summarizing Information page 256

2. The author believes that people need to think creatively
3. According to the article, a good computer hacker
4. So the author goes on to say that people
5. The author quotes one Internet user who
6. According to the list, the tenth most common password
7. And the article claims that the most common password
8. She describes a few things people

4 Avoid Common Mistakes

Editing Task pages 257-258

In his article "Privacy and Security Issues in Social Networking" (2008), Brendan Collins ~~looks into~~ *investigates* the security and privacy problems associated with social networks. He starts ~~off~~ by making the distinction between security issues and privacy issues, pointing out that social networking sites (SNSs) provide ideal opportunities for both types of violations to take place because they are so popular. As an example of a security violation, Collins cites the case of a hacker who shut down a social networking

site a few years ago just for fun. It was fortunate that the attack was harmless. If the attack had been committed with a malicious intent, the personal data of millions of users would have ~~be~~ *been* stolen. According to Collins, SNSs provide ideal opportunities for break-ins because they process so much information, and because so many people have access to them. As an example, he describes the case of Adrienne Felt, a PhD candidate at U.C. Berkeley, who ~~found out~~ *discovered/learned* that there was a security flaw in a major social networking site. In other words, the same program that allowed people to share photos and send invitations also exposed their information to theft. If Felt had not looked into the social networking site, a large proportion of users could have ~~get~~ *gotten* their information stolen. Collins goes on to recommend ways users can limit the possibility of security and privacy violations. Because SNSs are getting so big, he says, it is becoming impossible to monitor the activity that takes place on them. It is therefore the responsibility of users to take precautions as they share information about themselves. Collins concludes that there probably will never be a solution to these issues and implies that we will have to ~~put up with~~ *tolerate* threats to our privacy and security. Collins adds, however, that the less one uses SNSs, the lower the chance one has of getting their identity stolen.

5 The Writing Process
About Summary–Response Writing

Exercise

A page 259
Answers will vary.

B Pair Work page 259
Answers will vary.

Pre-writing Tasks

Choose a Topic

A page 260

Answers will vary.

B Pair Work page 260

Answers will vary.

Organize Your Ideas page 260

Answers will vary.

Writing Task page 261

Answers will vary.

Peer Review

A page 261

Answers will vary.

B page 261

Answers will vary.

18 Persuasion 1
Violence in the Media

1 Grammar in the Real World

A Before You Read page 262

Answers will vary; Possible answer: The writer believes that the government should regulate violence in media.

B Comprehension Check page 263

1. The author cites research by Brocato, et al. and a report by the FCC as evidence.
2. It might be difficult in the United States to regulate TV violence because it can conflict with the First Amendment.
3. *Answers will vary.*

C Notice

1 Persuasive Writing page 263

The following two arguments are emphasized in the essay: protect the public from overexposure to violence, help parents limit their children's exposure to violence.

2 Grammar page 263

1. The sentence referring to all children ("who have young minds that are easily impressionable") is on lines 25–26. The sentence identifying a particular group of children ("who watch violent TV shows and play violent video games") is on lines 6–7.

2. The relative clauses are not essential to understanding the sentences, but they give extra information about TV rating and program-blocking systems and about the Parents Television Council.

3 The Writing Process

Pair Work page 264

Possible answers:
1. The first sentence, "Should violence on TV be regulated?" is the hook. It is effective because it suggests conflict and makes the reader want to find out what the two sides of the argument are.
2. The writer introduces the issue of censoring violence in the media.
3. The writer uses evidence from two sources to support his or her position.
4. The writer's thesis is that the government should step in and regulate violence on TV.

2 Nonidentifying Relative Clauses
Exercise 2.1 Nonidentifying Relative Clauses

A pages 265–266

2. Expert: <u>the Philips Family Foundation</u>
   A child who watches two hours of TV a day is exposed to approximately 10,000 acts of violence a year, based on research by the Philips Family Foundation, which is a nonprofit organization that focuses on health-care issues.
3. Expert: <u>Joanna Moore</u>
   Parents should discuss the content of TV advertising with their children, according to Joanna Moore, who is the mother of five teenagers.
4. Expert: <u>Pablo Silva</u>
   According to Pablo Silva, who studies the effects of TV on children's development, the best way for children to be active is to turn off the TV set.
5. Expert: <u>The American Academy of Child & Adolescent Psychiatry</u>
   In 2006, the American Academy of Child & Adolescent Psychiatry, which provides resources about children's mental health, determined that children with excessive exposure to violence on television may "become 'immune' or numb to the horror of violence" (p. 1).
6. Expert: <u>Gerald Jones</u>
   Gerard Jones, who is a well-known comic book writer and the author of the article "Violent Media Is Good for Kids," believes that effective use of media violence can help children vent their anger.

B Pair Work page 266

Sentences 1, 2, 3, and 6.
2. A child who watches two hours of TV a day is exposed to approximately 10,000 acts of violence a year, based on research by the Philips Family Foundation, a nonprofit organization that focuses on health-care issues.

3. Parents should discuss the content of TV advertising with their children, according to Joanna Moore, the mother of five teenagers.
6. Gerard Jones, a well-known comic book writer and the author of the article "Violent Media Is Good for Kids," believes that effective use of media violence can help children vent their anger.

Answers will vary.

Exercise 2.2 More Nonidentifying Relative Clauses

A page 267

Possible answers:

2. Kevin McDonald, who has two children in elementary school, thinks Dr. Richards is right. He thinks violent cartoons caused his children to fight with each other.
3. Dr. Marcia Chan, who is a well-known child psychologist and author, doesn't think there's enough evidence to prove that kids are affected by cartoon violence.
4. Catherine Wong, who has two teenage boys, thinks each child has a different response to media violence.
5. Dr. Eric Lopez, who works at a children's hospital and has done a lot of research on the subject, believes that parents need to have firm rules regarding what's allowed and what's not.
6. Barbara Cramer, who is a spokesperson for No Violence Please, a nonprofit organization against media violence, thinks that as consumers, we need to actively protest against violence in the media.
7. Noah Friedman, who is a social worker, agrees with Dr. Lopez that parents must talk to their children and answer questions.

B Group Work page 267

Answers will vary.

3 Phrases That Limit Overgeneralization

Exercise 3.1 Words and Phrases That Limit Overgeneralization

A page 269

Possible answers:

2. Children are typically taught to deny their feelings of violence.
3. In most cases, adults attempt to repress any violent reactions they have. *OR* Adults typically attempt to repress any violent reactions they have.
4. According to some experts, media violence allows people to fantasize about releasing their aggression in a safe, nonthreatening environment.
5. Violent video games seem to provide players with an outlet for feelings of anger and frustration. *OR* It seems

that violent video games provide players with an outlet for feelings of anger and frustration.
6. Constant denial of violent feelings, rather than exposure to media violence, is likely to make people react to problems with aggression.
7. Video games tend to portray heroes as violent.

B Pair Work pages 269

Answers will vary.

4 Avoid Common Mistakes

Editing Task pages 270–271

There is a major reason that the government should not be involved in solving the problem of violence in the media. Government control of the media is unconstitutional. It ~~seem~~ *seems* that some people feel that the Federal Communications Commission (FCC), *which* is the government agency that regulates media such as TV and the Internet, is the best tool for protecting children. However, many experts disagree. For example, the American Civil Liberties Union (ACLU), ~~that~~ *which* focuses on constitutional rights, believes that government control of the media is a form of censorship. The First Amendment to the U.S. Constitution, *which* guarantees freedom of speech, gives us the right to media that are not controlled by the government. A free and open media is the foundation of democracy in the United States. However, it is important to protect children from violence. According to the ACLU, protecting children is the responsibility of parents, although it ~~seem~~ *seems* that many parents are unwilling to take on this responsibility. Caroline Fredrickson, *who* is a director of the ACLU's Washington Legislative Office, points out in her article, "Why Government Should Not Police TV Violence and Indecency," *which* was published in *The Christian Science Monitor* in 2007, that parents "already have many tools to protect their children, including blocking programs and channels, changing the channel, or simply turning off the television" (p. 2). She adds that the Parents Television Council, ~~that~~ *which* is a nonprofit media monitoring organization, provides information on their website about television programs that are appropriate for children. It ~~seem~~ *seems* that if parents take responsibility for monitoring their children's television viewing, then we will be able to have free and open media and protect children at the same time.

5 The Writing Process
About the Introductory Paragraph to a Persuasive Essay

Exercise

A page 271

Possible answers:
1. The topic of the essay is the attack on violence in video games.
2. Some adults believe that video games must be censored because they turn children into "mindless, heartless, killing machines," but many teenagers enjoy playing video games that include warfare and violence.
3. "There is a war out there, but it is not in any video game."
4. Adults' arguments and fears about video game violence are exaggerated and unnecessary.

B Pair Work page 272

Answers will vary.

Pre-writing Tasks
Choose a Topic

A page 272

Answers will vary.

B Pair Work page 272

Answers will vary.

Organize Your Ideas

A page 272

Answers will vary.

B Pair Work page 272

Answers will vary.

Writing Task page 273

Answers will vary.

Peer Review

A page 273

Answers will vary.

B page 273

Answers will vary.

19 Persuasion 2
Living in an Age of Information Overload

1 Grammar in the Real World
A Before You Read page 274

Answers will vary; Possible answer: Digital technology produces citizens who have fewer critical thinking skills and weaker social skills.

B Comprehension Check page 275

Possible answers:
1. The two main points in favor of technology mentioned by the writer are easy access to information and increased social connections.
2. Our critical thinking skills may become overloaded by the sheer volume of material to read when we do research online.
3. The choice between sharing a real flower and a "virtual" flower reflects the writer's point that technology can perhaps limit our personal interactions with the world.

C Notice
1 Persuasive Writing

Pair Work page 275

Possible answer: Writers include opposing views in their writing to show weaknesses in the opponent's views. Readers are more likely to be persuaded by an argument that includes opposing views because it shows a more balanced view.

2 Grammar page 275

1. "what they lose as well as what they gain" by technology
2. "While it is true that . . . " (lines 5–7)

3 The Writing Process page 275
b

2 Noun Clauses with *Wh-* Words and *If/Whether*
Exercise 2.1 Noun Clauses with *Wh-* Words and *If/Whether* page 277

2. Researchers are trying to determine whether/if information overload makes an employee more or less efficient.
3. Employers want to know what employees do when they are overwhelmed by too much information.
4. Employers wonder whether/if employees ignore important facts or absorb more when they are overloaded with information.

5. Corporations want to find out whether/if overloaded employees waste time.
6. Studies may determine how information overload affects employees' decision-making skills.
7. Researchers wonder when employees feel overwhelmed by information.
8. Researchers want to learn whether/if information overload increases or decreases productivity.

Exercise 2.2 More Noun Clauses with *Wh-* Words and *If/Whether*

A page 278

1. 5   6. 8
2. 2   7. 3
3. 9   8. 6
4. 4   9. 7
5. 1

B Pair Work page 278

2. what we can do about it
3. what some of the causes of information overload are
4. whether/if each recipient of information really needs the information that he or she receives
5. what the daily volume of new web content is
6. what you can do to avoid being overwhelmed by information
7. whether/if they can spend a portion of their day disconnected from technology
8. whether/if they have to look at that video that their friend sent them
9. whether/if they really need to send out e-mails to people who don't need them

3 Phrases for Argumentation

Exercise 3.1 Phrases for Argumentation
page 280

2. Unfortunately
3. Clearly,
4. while it is true that
5. Obviously
6. It could be argued that

Exercise 3.2 More Phrases for Argumentation
page 281

Answers will vary.

Exercise 3.3 More Phrases for Argumentation

Pair Work page 281

Answers will vary.

4 Avoid Common Mistakes

Editing Task pages 282–283

Opponents of online technology often point to the negative effects of the information age. They claim that *whether* ~~weather~~ individuals use the Internet for research or for social networking, they suffer from information overload. They believe that easy access to information has a negative effect on users' critical-thinking skills. They also cite the fact that online readers understand and retain less than print readers. The fact is, however, that experts have not yet determined if ~~or not~~ there is a difference between reading online and reading print material. There haven't been enough studies to determine if ~~or not~~ there truly are negative effects of information overload. Furthermore, it is important for proponents of this argument to identify *whether* ~~wether~~ they are referring to the effects of technology on older people or younger people. For example, their arguments may not be valid *if* ~~whether~~ they consider how digital natives respond to technology. Digital natives are people who were born since the 1990s. They were born into a digital world, and they have been using technology since childhood. According to Tapscott (2009), digital natives process information differently than digital immigrants (people who were born before the 1990s and learned how to use the Internet later in life than digital natives did). Tapscott cites a study designed to show whether digital natives retained more information from a traditional newscast or an interactive webcast. The study showed that digital natives remembered more from the interactive news source. Tapscott also points out that intelligence and aptitude test scores are rising, which further indicates that digital natives' thinking styles have not suffered. Some *whether* wonder ~~wether~~ digital natives should adapt to traditional ways of processing information. However, *whether* ~~if~~ or not we like it, the information age is here to stay. Therefore, digital immigrants are going to have to adapt to digital ways of interacting with technology.

5 The Writing Process
About Presenting and Refuting Opposing Views

Exercise page 284

1. c
2. d
3. a
4. b

Pre-writing Tasks

Choose a Topic

A page 284

Answers will vary.

B Pair Work page 284

Answers will vary.

Organize Your Ideas

A page 284

Answers will vary.

B Pair Work page 285

Answers will vary.

Writing Task page 285

Answers will vary.

Peer Review

A page 285

Answers will vary.

B page 285

Answers will vary.

20 Persuasion 3
Social Networking

1 Grammar in the Real World

A Before You Read page 286

Answers will vary; Possible answer: The writer thinks that social networking sites have a negative impact on students because they can be a distraction and online interactions are a less rigorous platform for ideas.

B Comprehension Check page 287

Possible answers:

1. It is possible to interact and maintain a relationship with someone without ever meeting in person; SNSs have created valuable ways to communicate and share information; students can create special interest groups and learn to communicate effectively in the digital age; and students often discuss current events and other issues that they normally wouldn't in the real world through SNSs.
2. The author wants to limit or ban SNSs on campuses because students waste valuable study time using SNSs and their grade point averages decline as a result.
3. *Answers will vary.*

C Notice

1 Persuasive Writing page 287

1. c
2. a
3. b

2 Grammar page 288

1. In line 7, *should* refers to a suggestion by the writer. In line 33, *should* refers to a conclusion drawn by the author that is a result of an action.
2. future time; *is likely to*
3. a likely result in the future

3 The Writing Process page 288

Name of Source	Information / Opinion Retrieved from Source
Smith, Rainie, Zickuhr	At least 85 percent of college students in the United States use online social networks daily.
Grabmeier	Students who do not use SNSs study 11 hours or more per week and have an average GPA between 3.5 and 4.0.
Hamilton	Teachers complain that students are "messaging friends or posting . . . status updates from their laptops instead of paying attention to lectures."

2 Expressing Future Actions
Exercise 2.1 Future Possibilities

A page 290

2. anticipate getting
3. is considering blocking
4. will have
5. hope to
6. seems likely
7. will
8. would
9. could

10. might
11. intend
12. are not likely

B Pair Work page 291

Answers will vary.

Exercise 2.2 Future Possibilities page 291

2. T

3. F; Lisa ~~is going to~~ *might* demonstrate against it if the school blocks access.

4. F; Ben ~~will~~ *won't* demonstrate against it if the school blocks access.

5. T

6. F; Lisa thinks a lot of people ~~might~~ *will* delete their account if the popular social networking site charges people.

7. F; Ben thinks that people ~~will~~ *might* pay to use the popular site.

8. F; Lisa ~~might~~ *wouldn't* use a social networking site if she has to pay.

3 Common Words and Phrases in Persuasive Writing

Exercise 3.1 Vocabulary in Persuasive Writing page 293

2. argue
3. Proponents; in favor of
4. Opponents
5. acknowledge
6. a valid point
7. against
8. evidence

Exercise 3.2 More Vocabulary in Persuasive Writing

Pair Work page 293

Answers will vary.

4 Avoid Common Mistakes

Editing Task pages 294–295

One of the main ~~arguing~~ *arguments* against social networking sites is that people sometimes reveal information on them that often should be kept private. Recently another development has provided more support for this ~~arguing~~ *argument*: College admissions committees are now using social networking sites as part of the application process. According ~~for~~ *to* a survey by Kaplan Test Prep (2010), over 80 percent of college admissions officers use social networking sites to communicate with students. The ~~claiming~~ *claim* that many colleges make is that they use these sites to attract new students or to stay in contact with former students. However, some colleges admit that they are also using social networking as part of the admissions process. The main ~~arguing~~ *argument* for using social media is that it helps colleges evaluate candidates at a time when these colleges are experiencing large numbers of applicants. According ~~with~~ *to* many admissions officers, colleges need all the information they can get on applicants in order to make decisions because the admissions process has become very competitive. One college interviewer in a recent survey reported that if she has to choose between two students who are equally qualified in terms of grades and test scores, she looks at their online profiles to make the final decision. In addition, applicants also use social networking sites against each other. According ~~for~~ *to* another admissions officer, his office often receives anonymous messages with links to sites that have negative information on or pictures of other applicants. Many colleges and universities do not have official policies yet on whether to use social media as part of the application process. Until these policies become clearer, prospective college students should keep their social networking pages private or remove anything that might make them look less attractive to admissions committees.

5 The Writing Process

About Writing Strong Arguments

Exercise page 296

1. c
2. a
3. b

Pre-writing Tasks

Choose a Topic

A page 296

Answers will vary.

B Pair Work page 296

Answers will vary.

Organize Your Ideas

A page 296

Answers will vary.

B Pair Work page 297

Answers will vary.

Writing Task page 297

Answers will vary.

Peer Review

A page 297

Answers will vary.

B page 297

Answers will vary.

Notes

Notes

Notes

Notes

Notes

Notes

Notes

Notes

Contents of the CD-ROM

Tests with Answer Keys

A ready-made Unit Test for each of the 20 units of the Student's Book is provided. The tests are easily scored, using a system found at the beginning of the Answer Key. Each Unit Test includes an optional writing section with a suggested rubric for scoring the writing. In addition, there is a Midterm and Final Test with Answer Key. These tests also include an optional writing section. Each test is available in both PDF and Microsoft Word formats. The placement test is also included on the CD-ROM.

Instructional PowerPoint Presentations

The PowerPoint presentations offer unit-specific grammar lessons for classroom use. The presentations include interactive versions of key *Presentations* for each unit.

Communicative Activities

Photocopiable Communicative Activities that expand lessons and offer additional contextualized practice of the grammar presented in the Student's Book.

Workbook Answer Key

Photocopiable answer key for all of the exercises in the Workbook is provided for easy reference.

CD-ROM Terms and Conditions of Use

This is a legal agreement between you ("the customer") and Cambridge University Press ("the publisher") for the *Grammar and Beyond 4 Enhanced Teacher's Manual CD-ROM*.

1. **Limited license**
   (a) You are purchasing only the right to use the CD-ROM and are acquiring no rights, express or implied, to the software itself, or the enclosed copy, other than those rights granted in this limited license for educational use only.
   (b) The publisher grants you the license to use one copy of this CD-ROM on your site and to install and use the software on this CD-ROM on a single computer. You may not install the software on this CD-ROM on a single secure network server for access from one site.

   (c) You shall not: (i) copy or authorize copying of the CD-ROM, (ii) translate the CD-ROM, (iii) reverse-engineer, alter, adapt, disassemble, or decompile the CD-ROM, (iv) transfer, sell, lease, lend, profit from, assign, or otherwise convey all or any portion of the CD-ROM, or (v) operate the CD-ROM from a mainframe system.

2. **Copyright**
   All titles and material contained within the CD-ROM are protected by copyright and all other applicable intellectual property laws, and international treaties. Therefore, you may not copy the CD-ROM. You may not alter, remove, or destroy any copyright notice or other material placed on or with this CD-ROM.

3. **Liability**
   The CD-ROM is supplied "as-is" with no express guarantee as to its suitability. To the extent permitted by applicable law, the publisher is not liable for costs of procurement of substitute products, damages, or losses of any kind whatsoever resulting from the use of this product, or errors or faults in the CD-ROM, and in every case the publisher's liability shall be limited to the suggested list price or the amount actually paid by the customer for the product, whichever is lower.

4. **Termination**
   Without prejudice to any other rights, the publisher may terminate this license if you fail to comply with the terms and conditions of the license. In such event, you must destroy all copies of the CD-ROM.

5. **Governing law**
   This agreement is governed by the laws of England, without regard to its conflict of laws provision, and each party irrevocably submits to the exclusive jurisdiction of the courts of England. The parties disclaim the application of the United Nations Convention on the International Sale of Goods.